THIS BOOK IS DEDICATED TO THE GLORY OF
GOD THE FATHER,
GOD THE SON, AND
GOD THE HOLY SPIRIT.

Contents

Preface

This book shares some insights of a decade of active witnessing, teaching, traveling, and experiencing the work and manifestations of our Lord the Holy Spirit in many places. Much of the material was intended originally to form a second part to Dennis' book, *Nine O'Clock in the Morning*, but it seemed better to leave that volume to deal exclusively with telling the story of the modern renewal of the Faith as it has touched our lives, and leave teaching and explanation for a separate book.

The part on Spiritual Gifts and the Fruit of the Holy Spirit is taken largely from *A Study Guide of the Spirit-Filled Life*, a booklet prepared by Rita to instruct those who receive the baptism in the Holy Spirit. This booklet has enjoyed wide circulation, and many who know it will welcome it in expanded form here.

The last ten years have been a decade of testimony, as the word of the baptism in the Holy Spirit has penetrated the "old-line" churches. Today thousands of ministers and priests of the older denominations have received the Holy Spirit as on the Day of Pentecost, as have millions of lay people. Now, while the testimony goes forward with ever-increasing strength, there is great need for teaching. Someone has pointed out that the return of the appetite to a sick person is one of the first signs of recovery. God's People have been very sick, nigh unto death, but now the Church of God is convalescent, and very hungry! We hope this book will help to supply some of the nourishment needed for a full recovery!

We, Dennis and Rita, are Episcopalians (Anglicans), but in this study it will be evident that we are not pushing any particular brand of Christianity. Our greatest desire is for people to meet the Lord Jesus Christ, and receive the power of the Holy Spirit, regardless of their denomination—if they have one. Occasionally we made references that would apply especially to our own denomination, or those similar, but the information we have given will also help others better understand these particular churches. We have dealt with the things that unite charismatic Christians, and have tried to avoid discussion of issues that have divided Christians through the centuries. The troubled questions are for the Holy Spirit to deal with, not us!

We do not claim or believe that we have all the truth, nor are we sure that in the coming years some of our views may not change, but we have presented these teachings sincerely and in the light we have at this time. During these years we have heard many outstanding speakers and teachers, and read numerous books on our subject. It would be impossible to give credit to all from whom the Lord has brought us knowledge and understanding. We can only thank the Holy Spirit Who has taught all of us. Where direct quotations are given throughout the book, we have, of course, given the source. Our most important written source, needless to say, has been Scripture itself. Also, we have learned many lessons through our own personal experiences.

We hope and pray that this book, *The Holy Spirit and You*, will be a help to many, both those who have been baptized in the Holy Spirit for years, and those just entering or getting ready to enter this area of Christian experience. We close with St. Paul's words:

"Grace be unto you, and peace, from God our Father, and from the Lord Jesus Christ. I thank my God always on your behalf, for the grace of God which is given you by Jesus Christ; That in every thing you are enriched by Him, in all utterance, and in all knowledge . . . So that you come behind in no gift waiting for the coming of our Lord Jesus Christ . . ." (I Cor. 1:3–5, 7).

Seattle, Washington
January 25, 1971

In the love of our Lord Jesus,
Dennis and Rita Bennett

1
The First Step

Several years ago, in one of the New England states, the wife of a Christian businessman, a friend of ours, was busy cleaning up the breakfast dishes when a knock came at the door. She opened it, to see her neighbor standing there—with a woebegone look on her face.

"I've just come over to say good-bye," the visitor announced. "We've been neighbors for quite a while, and although we don't know one another real well, I just wanted to let you know we're leaving."

"Why?" asked my friend's wife. "Has your husband got a new job, or what? Sit down. Tell me about it."

The neighbor dropped wearily into a chair. "No," she said, "nothing like that. We're losing the house—can't make the payments. Losing the car, too, for that matter." She opened her hands. lying in her lap, and stared at them. Then she looked up. "Might as well give you the whole story. John and I are getting a divorce."

"But, why? What in the world has gone wrong?"

"My husband and I are both hopeless alcoholics," said the woman sadly. "Just can't seem to shake it. Money's all gone, and everything else with it. What gets me the most is our child; I don't like to see him the victim of a broken home—and all that." The little woman was nearly in tears.

"But—," said my friend's wife, "don't you know there's an answer?"

The neighbor looked up abruptly: "What do you mean? We've tried everything we know! We just can't seem to stay on the program with AA. We've tried psychiatry, but even if that were a possible answer, we couldn't afford long-term counseling."

"Why don't you ask Jesus to help you?"

It was the neighbor's turn to look nonplussed. "Jesus? What's *He* got to do with it?"

"Why, He's the Savior!" exclaimed my friend's wife.

"Oh," said the visiting neighbor, "you mean religion and all that. Yeah, I'm religious. I mean, I believe in God, and I've tried to be a decent person." She laughed wryly. "I guess I haven't done too good a job of it though."

"No, no, that's not what I mean. I mean Jesus is a *savior*—He saves, rescues people. He'll rescue you from your situation, if you ask Him to take over. You do want out of it, don't you? I mean, you want to be different—to get things straightened out?"

The neighbor looked at her companion for a moment or two. "Never heard it put that way before," she said slowly. "You mean it's that simple?—just *ask* Him?"

My friend's wife nodded. "Uh-huh. He's alive, and He's right here. He'll do it!"

The neighbor sat for a moment or two in silence, then suddenly slipped out of the chair onto her knees and lifted her hands in a gesture of surrender. "I don't know how to say this," she said, "but, Jesus, please help me out of this mess. Please take over!" Then she stood up and without further comment, she went home.

Two days later the husband came over from next door. "What's happened to my wife?" he asked gruffly. "I want it, too!"

This Christian couple told him, and *he* got down on his knees on the kitchen floor and asked Jesus to take over *his* life!

What happened? The alcohol problem disappeared. It was only a symptom of their empty lives. The home was not lost. The marriage did not break up. Jesus *saves*—He saved their home, their marriage, their health, and probably their lives. Jesus isn't hesitant to start with people's immediate needs. Two of His great miracles were performed to provide hungry people with food. Almost all of His miracles were done to meet the physical needs of people. Often the first step in becoming a Christian is just a cry for help (Acts 2:21).

But more than that happened to the onetime alcoholic couple. Their whole way of life changed. They were different. Something happened to them *inside.*

The Greek word translated "save" in our English Bible is *sozo,* which means, according to the lexicon:

"*Sozo* . . . preserve or rescue from natural dangers and afflictions . . . save from death . . . bring out safely from a situation fraught with mortal danger . . . save or free from disease . . . from demonic possession . . . be restored to health, get well . . . keep, preserve in good condition . . . thrive, prosper, get on well . . . save or preserve from eternal death. . . ." [1]

To become a Christian doesn't mean to accept a philosophy, or a set of rules, or to believe a list of abstract principles; to become a Christian means to have God come and *live in you* (Col. 1:27).

To become a Christian is to *repent* (Acts 2:38; 26:18). That means to want to be different, to admit that you're on the wrong road and want to get right. Many come to Jesus, like the desperate couple in our story, because they know they're in a jam; they're heading for destruction. Jesus accepts them and meets their needs, if they are ready to change.

To become a Christian is to be *converted* (Acts 3:19; Matt. 18:3). This means turning around, and going in the opposite direction—the right direction—with Jesus.

To become a Christian is to be *forgiven* (Ps. 103:11–12). That

[1] W. F. Arndt and F. W. Gingrich, eds. *A Greek-English Lexicon of the New Testament and Other Early Christian Literature* (Chicago: University of Chicago Press, 1957).

means to have your sins really taken away, as though they had never existed—to have the record swept clean. More than that, it means to be able to be forgiven every day—to *live* forgiven! (I John 1:9).

To become a Christian is to be *born again* (John 3:1–21; I Peter 1:23), and here we get to the heart of the matter. An elderly scholar came to Jesus late one night looking for answers. Jesus said to him:

"Nicodemus, you've got to be born again!"

The old man shook his head. "How can I be born, when I'm grown up? Do I have to go back to my mother's womb and be born over again?"

Jesus answered: "Don't be silly, Nicodemus. You're a better scholar than that! I'm not talking about physical birth—that's already happened. You have to be born of the Spirit."

What did Jesus mean by this?

The Bible tells us that God created man with the ability to know Him and respond to Him. But at the very first, man broke that contact, and when he did, he died spiritually, and handed on that spiritual death to all his descendants. The very inmost part of us is called our "spirit," or *pneuma* in Greek, and this was created for one main purpose, to know God. An animal has a soul and a body, but a human being has a body, a soul, and a spirit (I Thess. 5:23). When man broke fellowship with God in the very beginning—what we call the fall of man—this inmost part died, or went out of action, and man ever since then has operated from his soul, and body (Gen. 2:17). No wonder we've gotten into such a mess! The "soul," called *psyche* in Greek, is the psychological part of us—composed of our intellect, our will, and our emotions. This part of us is wonderful, *when* it is under the control of God through the Spirit, but when it is out of control it does terrible things.

This is why human history is the record of hate, bloodshed, cruelty, and confusion; human beings are dead *spiritually*—

"dead in trespasses and sins" (Eph. 2:1 KJV) and trying to live *soulishly* while being out of touch with God and therefore lost (Luke 19:10). "Lost" means we don't know who we are, or where we are going, or what we are for. If this situation isn't corrected, it obviously means hell—it means that the person is going to be eternally lost, in the dark, frightened, rebellious, and hateful, separated from God forever; and not only that, but sharing in the endless destruction of the devil and his angels, for there is no "no-man's land." The great and desperate need, then, is to come alive, to get back in touch with God; and this is exactly what Jesus Christ is offering us. Through Jesus, and through Jesus alone— there is no other way—God's life can come and bring us alive (John 10:10).

However, the evil, which we committed while we were lost and out of touch with God, created a wall of sin and guilt which would keep us from receiving this new life (Isa. 59:2). God is love, but He is also justice. He cannot "let us off," any more than a just and loving human father could "let his son off" if he knew that he was guilty of a crime. The father would have to insist on the boy's "turning himself in" to the authorities. But if the boy was truly repentant, the father might then offer to pay the son's fine, serve his sentence, or even die in his place, supposing such a thing to be possible. Justice and love would then both be satisfied.

This is just what Jesus did. He met the requirements of justice by dying for us. Jesus was God in human Flesh—He was the Incarnation of the Second Person of the Godhead, the Creator God, by Whom the Father created the worlds (Eph. 3:9; Heb. 1:2). He was totally free from any sin or guilt. When Jesus died on the Cross, because He was God, and because He was innocent, He infinitely satisfied justice on behalf of all the sins that man had committed, or would ever commit.

In this way Jesus solved the problem of our guilt that was keeping us from the Father, and when He died and rose again, the way was open for the Father to send the Holy Spirit, through

Whom God's life was able to come and live in us. The only requirement is for us to see that we've been wrong, and to ask for forgiveness. Then we must ask Jesus to come and live in us and be our Lord and Savior. By the Holy Spirit, Jesus comes into our lives, our sins are washed away through His poured-out Blood, and we are given a new kind of life. The Holy Spirit having joined Himself to our spirit (I Cor. 6:17) brings it from death to life; it is "born again," and becomes what St. Paul calls a "new creature" (II Cor. 5:17; Rev. 21:4–5).

The new life created by the Holy Spirit in us, is what Jesus calls "eternal life." This doesn't just mean "going on and on," but *God's life* in us, the kind of life that never runs down, never gets tired, or bored, but is always joyful and fresh (I John 5:11).

When Jesus said that a little child was the greatest thing in the Kingdom of Heaven, He was making a comment on eternal life. A little child doesn't get tired of doing the same thing over and over. "Read it again, Mommy!" "Do it again, Daddy!" This continually renewed freshness and lack of boredom comes very close to expressing the kind of life God wants to give us. "Behold I make all things new!" Not just once, but continuously, says Jesus. He is the continual Renewer! We are promised that we shall walk in "newness of life," and this is the same thing as eternal life: continual refreshing, continual replenishing. The word "eternal" literally means "ageless"—never getting old.

Isaiah says, "They that wait upon the Lord shall renew their strength; they shall mount up with wings as eagles; they shall run, and not be weary; and they shall walk, and not faint" (Isa. 40:31 KJV).

How do you accept forgiveness and receive this new life?

1. Realize you've been lost and going in the wrong direction, and be willing to go God's way.

2. Admit that you've been wrong, and ask the Father to take away your guilt and sin by the Blood of Jesus.

3. Ask Jesus Christ, God's only begotten Son, to come into your life, and become your Savior and Lord (Rev. 3:20).

4. Believe He has come the minute you ask Him to. Thank Him for saving you and giving you the new life (I John 5:11–15).

Here is a simple prayer you might say if you have decided to receive Jesus:

"Dear Father, I believe that Jesus Christ is Your only begotten Son, and that He became a Human Being, shed His Blood and died on the Cross to clean away my guilt and sin that was separating me from You. I believe that He rose from the dead, physically, to give me new life. Lord Jesus, I invite You to come into my heart. I accept You as my Savior and Lord. I confess my sins, and ask You to wash them away. I believe that You have come and are living in me right now. Thank You, Jesus!"

When you pray this prayer, you may actually feel something happen, or you may not. Your "spirit" which comes alive through Jesus Christ is in a place far deeper than your emotions; therefore, sometimes there will be an emotional reaction, and sometimes not. Whether you feel anything immediately or not, you will find that you are different because Jesus will do what He has promised. Jesus keeps His Word. He said:

"Heaven and earth shall pass away, but my words shall not pass away" (Matt. 24:35 KJV).

2
The Overflow

If you have received Jesus as your Savior as described in the previous chapter, God is living in you. By the Holy Spirit He has joined Himself to your spirit. Your spirit, the very inmost part of you, is alive, and not only alive, but filled with all the wonderful joy, and love, and peace, and glory of God Himself.

"If any man be in Christ," says the Apostle Paul, "he is a new creature!" (II Cor. 5:17 KJV). He also says of Christians that they are seated in heavenly places with Christ (Eph. 2:6).

If you are like many people, you will say at this point:

"Well, I *am* different. Something certainly did happen to me when I invited Jesus into my heart, and for a while I had a deep sense of the love and joy you are talking about. I really wanted to tell everyone about it, too. But somehow, now, I seem to be cooling off. Life isn't all that different anymore. I still know that things have changed down inside me somewhere, but most of the time I feel just about as I did before. In the mornings, when I get away by myself and pray, I do sometimes feel God's presence, but I sure can't keep track of Him during the day!"

Why is this? It's not hard to understand if you will remember and take seriously what we said in the last chapter. In fact, many very difficult problems in Christian experience become understandable if you will accept what the Bible says about the nature of man, that you are a threefold being: spirit, soul, and body (I Thess. 5:23). If you are still thinking of yourself as two parts—soul and body—then you will inevitably confuse your psychological reactions with your spiritual life, and this is not only confusing to the understanding, it can actually, in this very psychological age, lead you into real false teaching. Many fine Bible teachers today, under the pressure of psychology, are identifying the spirit of man with the "unconscious mind," or the "deep psyche," simply because they do not take seriously the Bible's ability to divide between the soul and the spirit (Heb. 4:12). But if you make this division, you will not only be able to grasp what happens in the baptism in the Holy Spirit, but also will find yourself able to account for other things in your Christian life which may have puzzled you.

When you received Jesus as your Savior, your *spirit* came alive, began to assert its new life and take its rightful place as head over your *soul*—your psychological part (intellect, will, and emotions)—and your *body*, your physical part. Your body and soul, however, were accustomed to "running the show," and it wasn't long before they had pretty much overwhelmed your new life in the spirit, and resumed the driver's seat. When you pray in the morning, the busyness of your soul and body is quieted; your spirit has a chance to let you know he is there; and at this, and other times, you get an inkling that, deep inside you, the new life is very real. But as soon as the clamor of existence begins again, you automatically start to trust your soul and body rather than your spirit. You were so accustomed to living by your thoughts, feelings, and desires—by your soul, your psychological being—and by the demands of your body, that you soon lost track of the voice of the newly living spirit deep within you. It would seem that something needs to happen to your *soul* and *body* before your *spirit* can gain stronger control.

This "something" that needs to happen is that the Holy Spirit Who is living in your spirit needs to *flow out* to fill your soul and

body. This is described in the Scripture in a variety of ways. Just
as the experience of accepting Jesus is spoken of throughout the
Bible in different ways, so a number of descriptions are given of
the next experience: "baptism in (or with)[1] the Holy Spirit,"
"receiving the Holy Spirit," "Pentecost," "receiving power," the
Holy Spirit to "come upon" or "fall upon" a person. All these are
expressions of the same truth, viewed from different sides.

There is much difference of opinion over what terminology to
use. We don't want to erect any verbal barriers for anyone, so,
if using any one of these titles to refer to this second experience
disturbs you, why not call it "experience X-2," or something like
that? However, we feel on especially safe scriptural grounds using
the term "baptism in the Holy Spirit," since quite an impressive
list of biblical Persons so used it: God the Father (John 1:33),
God the Son (Acts 1:5), and God the Holy Spirit, Who is, of
course, the Inspirer of the Scriptures in which these expressions
are found; there were also John the Baptist (Matt. 3:11, Mark 1:8,
Luke 3:16, John 1:33), the four evangelists, Matthew, Mark,
Luke, and John, in the places just cited, and the Apostle Peter
(Acts 11:16). If you will read these references carefully, and
compare them, you will see in each case it is not salvation that is
spoken of, but a second experience.

This is called in the Scripture, "the baptism in the Holy Spirit,"
because it *is* a baptism, meaning a drenching, an overflowing, a
saturating of your soul and body with the Holy Spirit. When the
Bible speaks of Jesus "baptizing" in the Holy Spirit, we immediately visualize something external, somebody being *put into*
something. However, the word *baptize* in Greek means to "completely suffuse"—it is used in classical Greek of a sunken, water-
logged ship—so it does not really make any difference whether
Jesus immerses us in the Holy Spirit in an external sense of the
word; whether He inundates us from outside; or whether Jesus

[1] The Greek preposition *en*, used in this phrase, may be translated "in," or
"with."

causes the Spirit to rise and overflow from where He is living *inside* us, to suffuse our souls and bodies. Probably both pictures are true—He "comes upon us" both from outside and inside, but it is important to remember that the Holy Spirit is living *in* you, and that therefore it is from within that He can flood your soul and body. Jesus says:

"He that believeth on me . . . *out of* his belly shall flow rivers of living water [the Holy Spirit]" (John 7:38),[2] and the Amplified Bible says: *"Out of* his innermost being shall flow . . ."* When we receive Jesus as Savior, the Holy Spirit *comes in*, but as we continue to trust and believe Jesus, the Indwelling Spirit can *pour out* to inundate, or baptize, our soul and body, and refresh the world around.

This, too, is why again and again in Scripture the first normative evidence of this Pentecost experience is an *out*pouring:

"They were all filled with the Holy Ghost, and began to speak in other languages . . ." (Acts 2:4).

Some are puzzled by the term "receiving the Holy Spirit." A Christian may ask the question: "How can I *receive* the Holy Spirit when I already have Him living in me?" This expression can be understood easily if we remember that we are talking about a Person, not a thing or a quantity of something. Some have talked about the Holy Spirit in a quantitative way—as if you could receive *some* of the Holy Spirit at salvation, and some *more* at a later date. But if the Holy Spirit is a Person, which He is, then He is either living in you or He isn't.

We all know what it means to "receive" a person. Let us imagine the Brown household. It is 5:40 p.m., and Mr. Brown has just come home from work, and is taking a shower before supper. Mrs. Brown is putting the finishing touches on an especially nice meal, for the Browns have invited the Joneses over for dinner. Their guests are scheduled to arrive at 6:00 p.m., but alas, at

[2] Italics ours.

5:45 comes a ring at the doorbell. Mrs. Brown flutters a little— she isn't through with the gravy; she has flour on the end of her nose; and her hair is a mess!

"Susie!" she calls to her daughter, "for goodness' sake will you go and let the Joneses in; give them the evening paper, or visit with them—I'm not ready for them yet!"

Just then the phone rings in the kitchen, and Mrs. Brown answers.

"Hello! Marie?" says the voice on the line. "This is Helen. Do you have the Joneses over there?"

"Yes," replies Mrs. Brown, "we do."

"Well, how are they?" says the voice of the caller.

"I really don't know," says Mrs. Brown, patiently. "I haven't *received* them yet. I'm still out here working in the kitchen."

"You'd better hurry and receive them," says Helen. "I happen to know they have some wonderful news, and that they have brought you some beautiful gifts!"

So Mrs. Brown hangs up the phone, quickly finishes her cooking, straightens her hair and powders her face, and then, together with her husband, receives her friends, hears the news they have, and accepts the gifts they have brought. The Person of the Holy Spirit has been living in your "house" ever since your new birth, but now you fully acknowledge His Presence and receive His gifts.

Let us sum up, then, by saying that the first experience of the Christian life, salvation, is the *incoming* of the Holy Spirit, through Jesus Christ, to give us new life, God's life, eternal life. The second experience, is the *receiving*, or making welcome of the Holy Spirit, so that Jesus can cause Him to pour out this new life from our spirits, to baptize our souls and bodies, and then the world around, with His refreshing and renewing power. "Out of his belly shall flow rivers of living water!" The word used here is *koilia*, which refers quite literally to the physical body; it is by means of the physical body and its speech and actions that we contact our environment and the people around us. The world is not going to be helped or challenged until it sees and hears and experiences Jesus' life flowing from us.

Imagine an irrigation canal in Southern California, or some other area that is normally arid most of the year. The canal is dry, and so are the fields around. All the vegetation is dried up and dead. Then the gates from the reservoir are opened, and the canal begins to fill with water. First of all the *canal* itself is refreshed! The cool flow of water carries away debris and slakes the dust. Next, grass and flowers begin to spring up along the banks, and the trees on either side of the canal become fresh and green. But it doesn't stop there; all the way along the canal, farmers open the gates and the life-giving water pours out into the fields to make the "desert blossom as the rose."

So with you and me. The reservoir, the well, is in us when we become Christians. Then, when we allow the indwelling living water of the Spirit to flow out into our souls and bodies, *we* are refreshed first. Our minds come alive in a new way to God's reality. We begin to think of Him, even dream of Him, with a new frequency and joy. Our emotions respond, and we begin to be happy in Him. Our will responds, and we begin to want to do what He wants. Our bodies respond, not only by feelings of well-being, but by actual renewed strength and health and youth. Then the living water begins to pour out to others, and they see the power and love of Jesus in His people. He is now able to use us to refresh the world around us.[3]

---

[3] In the Episcopal, Lutheran, Orthodox, and Roman Catholic Churches the term "confirmation" is used of the traditional rite intended to confer this experience of the baptism in the Holy Ghost. "Confirm" literally means "to strengthen." The Episcopal Prayer Book says: "The Church provides the Laying on of Hands, or Confirmation, wherein . . . I receive the strengthening gifts of the Holy Spirit." This is made doubly clear by the selection from the Acts of the Apostles which is read at the confirmation service, namely, the story in Acts 8:14–17 of how Peter and John laid their hands on Philip's converts in Samaria so that they might "receive the Holy Ghost." Unfor-

tunately, the rite of confirmation, like so many things, tends to become just a formal action, with no real results expected; but in spite of that, one hears from people who at the time of the bishop's laying on of hands were really set free in the Spirit in a new way. One lady in Louisiana said to Dennis:

"I'm so glad that you came down here to tell us about all this. Twenty years ago, when the bishop laid his hands on my head, I just filled up with Something, and I began to speak in a new language! I didn't know what it was, and neither did the bishop!" That great saint of the early Pentecostal movement, Smith Wigglesworth, tells in his memoirs how he was confirmed in the Anglican Church at the age of nine, and how he was filled with the joy and the presence of the Lord for days, and could not understand why the other choir boys were not similarly inspired and changed! He also tells how, years later, the wife of an Anglican vicar laid her hands on his head and prayed for him to be baptized in the Holy Spirit, and at that time his experience was completed as he spoke in new languages and magnified God.

3

What Do the Scriptures Say?

This is the all-important question. No matter how cleverly we may work out our theories, if they don't agree with the Scriptures, they are unacceptable. What then was the work of the Holy Spirit among the early Christians in the New Testament?

First let us talk about Jesus Himself. If anyone was indwelt by the Holy Spirit it was the Lord Jesus. He was *conceived* by the Holy Spirit, that is, His physical birth was by the direct action of the Holy Spirit. He was the Incarnation of the Word of God. By the Holy Spirit's action, God's only Son, the Creative Word, Who was from all eternity with the Father, and by Whom the worlds were created, took upon Himself a human Soul and Body. When He did this, however, He set aside His power, that is, He temporarily accepted the limitations of natural humanity (Phil. 2:7–8).[1] His human body, although perfect, was really and truly human, with all the limitations of a natural body. His Soul, His psychological being, although perfect, was subject to limitations, too. The Bible tells us that "Jesus *increased* in wisdom [in His Soul] and stature [in His Body], and in favour with God and man" (Luke 2:52 KJV). He subjected Himself to growth and development as a human child. The foolish stories in some of the Apocryphal "Gospels" about Jesus working fantastic mir-

[1] Literally: "He emptied Himself."

acles as a child—turning clay sparrows into live ones, striking His playmates dead and then bringing them to life again—are just that—foolish stories. The early believers recognized them as such and by the wisdom of the Holy Spirit kept them out of the approved Scriptures. Rather we see from the Scriptures that Jesus lived in Nazareth until He was thirty years old, and no one had any idea that He was God come in the Flesh. Even His mother Mary had only an inkling. How do we know this? Because when He did begin His ministry, His mother was amazed and worried about Him; and His own brothers and sisters did not believe in Him. The people of the village where He was brought up said:

"Who does He think He is? We know *Him;* He's the carpenter's Son!" They were so indignant that they actually tried to kill Him (Matt. 13:54–58; Luke 4:16–30).

What was it that happened to Jesus between the time that He was living in the village of Nazareth, and functioning as the village carpenter (stonemason and blacksmith, too, probably), and the time when He suddenly went out and began to proclaim: "The Kingdom of Heaven has come near!" and to heal the sick, and cast out devils, and even raise the dead, in proof of His claim to come from God, and to be God's Messiah-King? The answer is plain enough: "He received the power of the Holy Spirit." He was born of the Holy Spirit from the start, but when He began His ministry at the age of thirty, the Holy Spirit came on Him in a new way. You can read in all four of the Gospels, how John the Baptist saw the Holy Spirit descend and remain on Jesus. Jesus was the Father's only begotten Son from all eternity, long before the crowd at Jordan heard the Voice of God as He spoke from Heaven acknowledging His Son. So also the Holy Spirit was in Jesus from the beginning of His life on earth, long before John the Baptist saw the Spirit like a Dove come down upon Him. Nevertheless, following this, the Spirit began to be manifested through Jesus with new power. His ministry began. The Spirit led Him into the wilderness to be tempted by the Devil, and after His victory there, we read: "Jesus returned *in the power of the Spirit* into Galilee; and there went out a fame of Him through all the region round about" (Luke 4:14 KJV). Why was the full manifestation of the Holy Spirit held back until this point? One reason was so that Jesus could lead a normal everyday life in Nazareth without being detected as a very special Person. The Father kept His Son concealed, so to speak, until He was ready to reveal Him to the world. It seems likely that the Devil himself was deceived by this. It was not until Jesus was revealed in the full power of the Spirit that Satan confronted him. We may see Herod's attempt on Jesus' life in his infancy as an earlier effort on Satan's part to get rid of the Son of God, but it really seems even more likely that the prince of darkness was not fully aware of Jesus until He was baptized in the Holy Spirit.

Another reason for the delay was in order that Jesus could show us by His example what was supposed to happen to *us*. The Baptizer in the Holy Spirit was Himself baptized in the Holy Spirit.

John the Baptist had been told by the Father that the One upon Whom he saw the Spirit descend and remain would be the One Who would baptize in the Holy Spirit (John 1:33). It may well be that this is why John said to Jesus: "I need to be baptized by You, and You are coming to me!" (Matt. 3:14). Although he said this before the actual descent of the Spirit upon Jesus, John could well have prophetically perceived that Jesus was to be the Baptizer in the Holy Spirit.

Baptism with water in the Name of the Father, Son and Holy Ghost, or in the Name of Jesus—both are used in the New Testament—seems to have been universal in the early Church, as the "outward and visible sign" of the "inward and Spiritual grace" of salvation and new life in Christ. It is assumed that you who are reading this book and who accept Christ, will receive or have received baptism with water in the manner of the particular Christian fellowship to which you belong, and in accordance with your understanding of what the Scripture teaches about it. Notice clearly, however, that baptism with water is the outward sign of baptism *into* Jesus (salvation) (I Cor. 12:13), but not the baptism *by* Jesus into the Holy Spirit (Pentecost) (Luke 3:16). Perhaps this is the reason that Jesus Himself did not baptize anyone with water during His ministry on earth, although He must have instructed his disciples to do so even before his crucifixion. John 4:1 says: "When therefore the Lord knew how the Pharisees had heard that Jesus made and baptized more disciples than John, (though Jesus Himself baptized not, but His disciples,) He left Judaea, and departed again into Galilee." Perhaps Jesus refrained from performing water baptism Himself in order to make it clear that He had another baptism to bring—that He was to baptize "with the Holy Ghost, and with fire."

No doubt one of the reasons John's converts followed Jesus is that they heard that Jesus had another baptism to give them. They must have expected it to be a wonderful experience from the way John spoke about it, and that this experience would be just as clear and positive as their baptism with water had been. They were probably expecting it to happen at any time, but instead, as they followed Jesus, He did miracles, and healed the sick, was crucified, and resurrected from the dead, but still no one was baptized with the Holy Spirit!

After Jesus had died and risen from the dead, He appeared to His disciples the very evening after His resurrection, and conferred on them the *new life in the Spirit* which we talked about in the first chapter (John 20:22). The Holy Spirit came to live in them, bringing their spirits to life—they were "born again of the Spirit" just as you have been if you have accepted Jesus as Savior. This new birth for us corresponds to the fact that Jesus was "conceived by the Holy Ghost," so your spirits are born again of the Holy Spirit. Jesus had not yet finally ascended to take His place "on high" with the Father, so He could not yet pour out the Holy Spirit "upon all flesh," but He could and did confer Him individually to come and dwell in His first chosen ones. He told them that there was a further experience for them, and that they were to wait for it. His final words to them at the Ascension were to remind them of this.

If you were given a chance to say some final words to your friends and family before departing from them for a long time, they would be well-chosen words, we may be sure! Jesus chose His final words well. His most important message had been "You must be born again," but now that His followers had received the new birth, He gave them the next important instruction: "Wait until you receive the Power!" (Luke 24:49).

"John baptized you with water," He said, "but you will be baptized with the Holy Ghost not many days hence" (Acts 1:5). The believer follows the pattern that Jesus has set. The new birth in the Spirit corresponds to Jesus' being conceived by the Holy Ghost. The believer is baptized with water as Jesus was. After this, we are to expect to be baptized in the Holy Spirit, receiving the power of the Spirit as He did.

So these believing, born-again followers of Jesus, 120 of them, waited, as He had told them. They were praising God, praying, going to the Temple; they even had a business meeting and an election! (Acts 1:15–26). We do not read, however, that they were telling anyone else about Jesus. The power to do that effectively would come on the day of Pentecost.[2] Jesus had told them: "You will receive power, after the Holy Ghost is come upon you, and you will be witnesses of Me, both in Jerusalem, and in all Judaea, and in Samaria, and unto the uttermost parts of the earth" (Acts 1:8). A "witness" is not just someone who sees something happen,

---

[2] Without question there are Christians who do not claim a "Pentecost experience" yet witness effectively; but how much more effective they could be if they received the full release of the Spirit. The most characteristic evidence of the revival of Pentecost is a tremendous increase in Christian witness, resulting in a worldwide spiritual renewal that has been gaining momentum continuously for nearly a hundred years.

but someone who is ready and willing to *say* he saw it happen! This is why our English word "martyr" is the Greek word for "witness"!

Ten days after Jesus had left them to return to the Father, on the Feast of Pentecost, the Feast of the First-Fruits, the Power came, with the sound of a "rushing mighty wind," with flames like fire, and the disciples were all "filled with the Holy Ghost and began to speak with other tongues, as the Spirit gave them utterance" (Acts 2:4 KJV). It is important to remember that the Holy Spirit *was already living in them*, ever since Jesus had conferred on them new life in the Spirit on the evening of the resurrection. This new life was the Holy Spirit joined to their spirits. "He that is joined unto the Lord is one Spirit" (I Cor. 6:17 KJV), says Paul, and he also says: "If any man have not the Spirit of Christ, he is none of his" (Rom. 8:9 KJV). Now, on the Feast of Pentecost, the Father, through the ascended Lord Jesus at His right hand, shed forth the Holy Spirit from "on high," *upon all flesh*; that is, the new birth, new life in Christ, is now available to all who call upon Him. The Holy Spirit has come. God has made Himself available to man in a new way. "The Kingdom of Heaven has come near!" But, as the Holy Spirit was poured out upon the whole human race, so He was stirred *within* those first followers—He had been dwelling in *them* ever since Jesus had specially conferred Him on the evening after the Resurrection—and He began to pour forth from them in mighty manifestations of power. He overwhelmed them—this is what the Scripture means when it says He "fell upon them," or "came upon them"—baptizing their souls and bodies in the power and glory that was already dwelling in their spirits. This second experience, the *outpouring* of the Holy Spirit, would happen to others who received Jesus, too, but here again the first chosen followers, the one-hundred-and-twenty, were allowed to receive first. He overflowed from them out into the world around, inspiring them to praise and glorify God, not only in their own tongues, but in new languages, and in so doing, tamed their tongues to His use, freed their spirits, renewed their minds, refreshed their bodies, and brought power to witness. A great crowd gathered, baffled by the sound of these Galileans speaking the praises of God in languages of far-off countries. The listeners were not foreigners, but devout Jews from all over the world (Acts 2:5). They had come "home" for the great Feast Day. They were amazed to hear these humble people praising God in languages they knew they could not have learned, languages of the countries where the listeners had been brought up, and other tongues which they did not recognize, "tongues of men and of angels" (I Cor. 13:1 KJV).

Some jeered, and said: "They're just drunk, that's all!" but Peter responded: "No, they're not drunk! After all, it's only nine o'clock in the morning! But *this is that* which was prophesied by Joel: . . . In the last days, says God, I will pour out of My Spirit upon all flesh" (Acts 2:13–17). So convincing were the signs, that three thousand of those "devout men" accepted Jesus as Messiah, repented of their sins, were baptized, and themselves received the gift of the Holy Ghost that day.

It's funny that even some outstanding Bible scholars will say: "Pentecost happened only once," when very clearly there are a series of "Pentecosts" in the New Testament. The next one takes place in Samaria. The Samaritans were the remnant of the Israelite Northern Kingdom. They and the Jews, the people of the Southern Judaean Kingdom, were still at loggerheads. They hated one another heartily. In Acts 8, however, we read how Philip— not the Apostle, but one of the seven men appointed to help the apostles (Acts 6:1–6)—had gone to Samaria, and was telling the Samaritans about Jesus. It was an unlikely territory, but the Samaritans listened to Philip, although he was a Jew proclaiming a Jewish Messiah, because they saw him doing the works of power that Jesus had done, and they heard him speaking with authority, just as Jesus had spoken. The Holy Spirit in Philip impressed the Samaritans with the truth and reality of what he was saying, and they accepted Jesus, were born again of the Spirit, and baptized with water (Acts 8:5–12).

When the apostles at Jerusalem heard of this new breakthrough in Samaria, they sent Peter and John to see what was taking place. As soon as these two arrived, they saw something lacking. The Holy Spirit wasn't "falling upon" or overwhelming these new believers. Peter and John didn't doubt that the Samaritans had been born again of the Spirit, but they were concerned that the Spirit had not yet "fallen upon" or overwhelmed them; so they "laid . . . their hands on them, and they received the Holy Ghost" (Acts 8:14–17 KJV). Notice that Peter and John expected that the Holy Ghost would already have "fallen upon" the Samaritan converts. As a matter of fact, this is the first time we are told of any laying on of hands to receive the Holy Spirit. We are not told of any laying on of hands for the 3000 converted on Pentecost, and of course the first 120 had no laying on of hands. Later in this same chapter, we don't read of Philip laying hands on the Ethiopian Eunuch (Acts 8:27–40). We may presume that often the overwhelming or baptism of the Holy Spirit followed spontaneously after salvation, just as it did later to Cornelius at Caesarea Philippi (Acts 10:44). But here Peter and John felt that a laying on of hands was necessary to encourage the Samaritans to receive the Holy Spirit. The Holy Spirit was already indwelling these Samaritan believers. He was ready to inundate their souls and bodies, to baptize, to overflow, but they had to respond, to receive. As soon as they did, the Holy Spirit began to pour out from them just as He had with the first believers on the Day of Pentecost. Undoubtedly they gave the same sign, speaking in new languages and glorifying God. The Scripture does not specifically say so, but the major commentators agree that this is what happened. The solid and conservative Matthew Henry says, for example:

"It is said (v. 16), The Holy Ghost was as yet fallen upon

none of them, in those extraordinary powers which were conveyed by the descent of the Spirit upon the day of pentecost. They were none of them endued with the gift of tongues, which seems then to have been the most usual immediate effect of the pouring out of the Spirit. . . . This was both an eminent sign to those that believed not, and of excellent service to those that did. This, and other such gifts, they had not, only they were baptized in the name of the Lord Jesus, and so engaged in him and interested in him, which was necessary to salvation, and in this they had joy and satisfaction (v. 8) though they could not speak with tongues. . . .

"They laid their hands on them, to signify that their prayers were answered, and that the gift of the Holy Ghost was conferred upon them; for, upon the use of this sign, they received the Holy Ghost, and spoke with tongues." [3]

One observer, at any rate, was deeply impressed: Simon Magus, the sorcerer, who had been deceiving the people of Samaria with his black magic for many years. He rushed up to Peter with gold in his hand, and said:

"Look here, I'll make you rich, if you'll just tell me how you did that! Give me the power, so that when I lay hands on someone he will receive this Holy Ghost!" (Acts 8:18–24). Peter of course, told Simon off very firmly—the Gift of God was not to be bought for money—but still the question remains: "What did Simon see?"

On this occasion it says that by "the laying on of the apostles' hands the Holy Ghost was given" (Acts 8:18 KJV) and this has led some to claim that the Holy Spirit was *distributed* by the apostles: the Samaritans couldn't receive the Holy Spirit until Peter and John arrived from Jerusalem to "give" Him, since Philip, who was not an apostle, could not do so. This, however, does not match the rest of the Scripture. We have already pointed out that

[3] Matthew Henry, *Commentary on the Whole Bible* (New York: Revell), VI, 100.

in some cases of receiving the Holy Spirit we hear of no laying on of hands at all.

Also when Paul received the Holy Spirit, although he did have hands laid on him, they were the hands of an otherwise unknown man of whom the Scripture says only: "There was a certain disciple . . . named Ananias" (Acts 9:10 KJV). Although the Scripture does not record at this place that Paul spoke in tongues, we know that he did so from I Corinthians 14:18 (RSV): "I thank God I speak in tongues more than you all."

The next "Pentecost" in the Acts of the Apostles took place in the town of Caesarea which was a center of the Roman occupation forces. Here a devout Roman officer named Cornelius, who believed in God with all his heart, was told by an angel to send and ask Peter, who was staying at Joppa, an ultra-Jewish community on the seacoast, to come and tell him what he ought to do (Acts 10:6).

Peter naturally would not have wanted to go to tell Roman soldiers about Jesus, and the baptism in the Spirit. Up to this point it was thought that the new birth and the baptism in the Holy Spirit were for Jewish believers only. If a Gentile, a non-Jew, wanted to receive Christ and the Holy Spirit, he must first become a Jew—and come under all the difficult requirements of the Jewish Law. The Holy Spirit, however, made it very clear to Peter, by a series of visions, and by direct instructions, that he was to go with the Romans when they invited him, and he did (Acts 10:9-23). To Peter's amazement, when he arrived at Cornelius' house, and began to tell the Romans gathered there about Jesus, they immediately responded. The first thing Peter and his companions who had come with him saw and heard was these Romans, filled with joy, speaking in tongues, and magnifying God! (Acts 10:24-48). They had opened their hearts to Jesus, He had given them new life in the Spirit, and they immediately allowed that new life to fill them and overflow. Peter and his friends were amazed, but recognized right away that God was "pouring out His Spirit on the Gentiles," first in salvation and next in the baptism in the Holy Spirit. So Peter said: "Who can hinder us from baptizing these people with water, since they have received the Holy Ghost just as we did?" (Acts 10:47). Defending himself when they returned to Jerusalem against the criticism leveled at him for baptizing non-Jews, Peter said:

"In my beginning to speak to them (the Romans), the Holy Ghost overwhelmed them, even as with us at the beginning. And I remembered the word of the Lord, how He said 'John indeed baptized with water, but you shall be baptized with the Holy Spirit!' If then God gave to them the like gift as also to us, who believed on the Lord Jesus, who was I to be able to withstand God?" (Acts 11:15–17).

Notice Peter speaks of the gift of the Holy Spirit given to *those who believed*, which makes it clear that the Romans first *believed*, and then the Spirit "fell upon" or overwhelmed them.

We must wait thirty years for the next example in the Acts of a "Pentecost." Perhaps the Holy Spirit left just such a gap in order to show that these things did not die out. Paul is making his second visit to Ephesus, when he is greeted by a group of twelve men who claimed to be disciples. He immediately misses something in them, for he asks them:

"Didn't you receive the Holy Ghost since you believed?" (Acts 19:2). Again we see that the experience of salvation was expected to be followed by the baptism in the Spirit, but that the early Christian recognized that there *could* be a delay—otherwise why would Paul have bothered to ask the question? Rather, he would have questioned their *salvation*.

"We haven't even heard if there *is* a Holy Spirit!" (Acts 19:2), replied the Ephesians. Upon investigating further, Paul found that they didn't even know about Jesus, so he led them to accept Jesus, baptized them with water, and then we read: "When Paul had laid his hands upon them, the Holy Ghost came on them, and they spoke with tongues, and prophesied" (Acts

19:6). Here again the distinction is clear. They received Christ, were baptized with water as the outward sign; then, encouraged by Paul's laying on of hands, they responded to the Holy Spirit Who had come to live in them, and began to pour out the praise of God in new languages.

We have tried to show in this chapter the scriptural pattern of what the writer of the Book of Hebrews calls the "doctrine of *baptisms.*" The Apostle Paul, in Ephesians 4:5 says there is "one Lord, one faith, one baptism," yet it is clear that in the New Testament this "one baptism" divides into three. In I Corinthians 12:13, Paul says: "In one Spirit we were all baptized into one Body . . . and were all made to drink into one Spirit." This refers to the spiritual baptism into Christ which takes place as soon as Jesus is received as Savior. This was followed by the baptism with the Holy Spirit, in which the now indwelling Holy Spirit poured forth to manifest Jesus to the world through the life of the believer. Either before or after the baptism with the Holy Spirit there was the outward sign of baptism with water— symbolic of the inner cleansing by the Blood of Jesus, the death of the "old man," and the resurrection to new life in Christ.[4] To which of these three baptisms is Paul referring as the "one baptism"?

An artist can look at a picture he has been painting in different ways. He may look to make sure it is a balanced composition; he may look again to check lighting effects of the sunlight on the water and the trees; again he may view it from a different point of view as he checks perspective. We have been looking at the different aspects of God's saving work in man. It is necessary to look at these three experiences—salvation, water baptism, and Pentecost—separately, because in our inhibited way of living they

[4] The normative pattern in the New Testament was to accept Jesus, receive water baptism, and be baptized with the Holy Spirit. However, in two of the five accounts in Acts, they accepted Jesus, were baptized with the Holy Spirit, and then baptized with water.

have become separated, and the full picture has been lost. In the early church, the three experiences in each life occurred closely together—but this has not often been the case today.

Having viewed the picture in different ways during our study, we now need to step back and see it as a whole. Paul says there is "One Lord"—yet the Godhead is Three in One: Father, Son, and Holy Ghost. Man is one, yet he is a trinity of body, soul, and spirit. The Body of Christ on earth is one, yet composed of many members. So when Paul speaks of "one baptism," it would seem he is speaking of the composite action by which Jesus Christ comes to live in us, the outward sign by which this action is sealed, and the overflow of the Holy Spirit through us to minister to the lost world.

We recommend to you that, even though you may have difficulty with these things in your mind, you come and experience God's reality in the fullness of the Spirit. Intellectual understanding will come later. As the great St. Augustine of Hippo put it: *"Credo ut intelligam,"* that is, "I believe in order that I may understand."

4

Preparing to Receive the Baptism
in the Holy Spirit

The Holy Spirit comes to live in us when we receive Jesus, and
are born again of the Spirit. The baptism in the Holy Spirit
is the *pouring out* of the Spirit. We cannot very well expect Him
to pour out through us until He is living in us, so before we ask
to be baptized in the Holy Spirit, we must first be sure that we
have indeed received the Lord Jesus as Savior, and invited Him
to live in us by His Spirit.

Jesus is the Way to God. There isn't any other. He is the only
Way by which we can know God or receive His life. Jesus Christ
is fully and truly God and fully and truly Man. This is the meaning of the Incarnation—God really and truly became Man in
the womb of the Virgin Mary. Thus Jesus is the Meeting-Point
of God and Man.

There are other philosophies and religions that attempt to tell
about God, and some of the things they say are true, but if you
want God Himself to come to you and live in you, you can *meet*
Him only through Jesus Christ. *Whatever you do, do not pray to
be "baptized in the Holy Spirit" unless you have received Jesus
Christ as your Savior personally, or you may get into serious
spiritual confusion.*

Someone will usually say at this point:

"But what about people who have never heard of Jesus? What about the members of other cultures and other religions? Will they all be lost just because they have never heard?" We can only reply:

1. No one will be in the Kingdom of Heaven except through Jesus Christ.

2. For those born since Jesus Christ came to this world, the decision is made in this present life. *There is no opportunity to accept Christ after death* (Heb. 9:27).

3. God has ways of reaching people in this life that we know nothing about. We can hope that God is able in some way to offer the opportunity to know Jesus to all who would accept Him if they did meet Him. We know that God wants everyone to come to Him, and takes no "pleasure in the death of a sinner" (Ezek. 33:11). God, however, although He is all-powerful and all-knowing, has limited Himself in His dealings with men, by *really* giving us free will.

4. The real answer to the person who feels it would be terrible for any human being not to have the opportunity to know Jesus, is that Jesus was concerned about this, too, and gave the answer: "Go all over the world and tell everybody!" (Mark 16:5).

Christians have so sadly failed to do this (one responsible survey recently showed that ninety-five percent of all Christians have never told anyone else about the Savior) that many intelligent and spiritually hungry people are looking for answers in the wrong places. Many have become involved with the beliefs usually called the "cults," while others are investigating the "occult."

In general, the term "cult" is used of religious groups that teach some other way to God than Jesus Christ, and/or whose teachings add to, subtract from, or contradict those of the Holy Scriptures. Most cults teach that Jesus Christ is something less than personally God. Some cults have been around for a long time, and have acquired a lot of status, often being regarded as "churches," but that does not change their situation; it just makes them more dangerous.

We are not going to try to deal with the cults by name; it is wrong *teachings* we are concerned about, not personalities, names, or titles. Adherents of the cults many times are fine and well-meaning people, devoted zealously to their cause, for which they are ready to make real sacrifices. Their human attitudes and behavior are sometimes better than those of many who claim to be orthodox believers.

The first such erroneous teaching we will name is that of several of the best-known cults; we may call it "mind-science." This teaches that God is "universal mind," that "mind" is the only reality, and that we will be "saved" by getting our *thinking* straightened out. Thoughts and ideas are the only real things, they say; matter is not real; sickness is not real; sin is not real; these things are just "error of mortal mind." Jesus of Nazareth, they say, was not a divine Person; He was a human being Who was greatly filled with the "Christ Spirit." We, too, can be filled with the "Christ Spirit" and be like Jesus. (The "Christ Spirit" turns out to be a kind of generalized spirit of love and goodwill between persons.) Jesus is called the "Way-Shower," instead of the Way. Obviously there is no need for forgiveness of sins, just corrected thinking. There is no need for healing, since sickness is not real, and will disappear as soon as the wrong thoughts are corrected.[1]

---

[1] The question is often asked whether the "healings" that allegedly take place as a result of this philosophy are "Christian" healings. The answer is obvious. Christians accept the fact that people get sick. Sickness is the work of Satan. Jesus Christ cures sickness. That is Christian healing, and it leads people to Jesus as Savior, not only of their bodies, but of their souls and spirits. The "mind-science" groups, on the other hand, believe the person is not sick at all, but just has wrong thoughts. Once these thoughts are corrected, the apparent illness disappears. This has nothing whatsoever to do

One of the strongest of these "mind-science" groups, that puts out a great deal of prayer literature, and has a strong following among church people, also teaches *reincarnation*. This false teaching is also being popularized very widely by another recent cult organized around the doings of a skillful clairvoyant, who claimed a strong ability to diagnose disease by psychic means. *Reincarnation* is the belief that we are born over and over again in other bodies on this earth to continue our spiritual growth, and to expiate our sins. Untold thousands are being deceived by this teaching, again many of them being from the "old-line" churches.

There is no place for a belief in reincarnation among Christians. It is totally unbiblical and anti-Christian. The Scripture says: "It is given to all men *once* to die, and after that the judgment (Heb. 9:27).

The teaching of the Scripture is that in God's Kingdom we shall meet and know one another, happy forever in a fellowship never again to be broken. For instance, when I meet my mother in heaven, is it to be as someone else, after fifty or so "reincarnations"? How ridiculous!

The teaching of reincarnation is usually accompanied by the so-called law of karma, which says we must be born over and over again to expiate our sins, and to work out our own salvation. It says our troubles in this life are caused by our sins of past lives; sin can be eliminated only by our living over again and receiving punishment for it. This is a million miles from the good news that Jesus died on the cross to take away our sins.

Another powerful 'cult, often accepted as a true variety of Christianity, claims to be the only true "church," that all others are false. It teaches that God the Father was, and is, a man, a being of "flesh and bone," who became an "almighty god." It

---

with Jesus Christ. There was no disease, so there could have been no healing. There certainly was not witness to the Saviorhood of Jesus, nor are people led to acceptance of Jesus as Lord.

also teaches that men, if they will keep the teachings of the cult, can become "almighty gods," and have their own planets to rule, which they will people with their "spirit children" that they have begotten by their many "spirit wives"! Rather obviously, one of the first requirements for full salvation in this cult is that you get married! Jesus died on the cross, this group tell us, to bring all men to the point where they could save themselves by keeping the teachings of this particular cult. This group, like others, teaches that the Bible is not sufficient to show the way of salvation; it must be supplemented by other books and writings. In fact, the most important teachings of this cult are not drawn from the Bible at all, but from their special books—one of which was supposedly discovered written on "golden plates" and buried, and others written by "prophets" through the years. Many people are drawn to this cult because of a strong social welfare emphasis.

Yet another of the strongest cults, one that distributes its literature on the street corners, and assiduously calls at homes offering "Bible study," denies the threefold nature of God (the Trinity), saying that Jesus was not God come in the flesh, but a kind of "in-between" being, *a* god. This group, like others, has its own translation of the Scriptures, slanted to support its own peculiar doctrines.

Most cults deny the bodily resurrection of Jesus. They say His "resurrection" was the appearance of His "spirit" only. This, of course, is in flat contradiction to Jesus' own statement on the evening of the resurrection when He appeared to His friends: "Touch Me and see that it is I Myself! A spirit doesn't have flesh and bones, as you see that I do!" (Luke 24:39).

The cults would naturally deny the real, physical "second coming" of Jesus to the earth.

Another kind of cult is the "eclectic." This teaches that we must accept the "good" in all religions; that Jesus of Nazareth was just one among many "great teachers." Along with this often goes the claim that another "great teacher" has arisen to take Jesus' place! The basic error here is the idea that religion is a "search for truth," and that Jesus was just one among many "teachers of truth." (This is the teaching of most "comparative religion" courses in our colleges and universities.) Christianity, however, is not a search for abstract and metaphysical "truth," but an entering into a new relationship with God: new life. Christianity teaches that God is reaching down to man: "The Son of Man is come to seek and to save that which was lost" (Luke 19:10).

You can easily see, from what we have said so far, that the cults either deny that Jesus is divine at all (except in the sense that "all men are divine," and Jesus may be a little ahead of the rest!), or they deny that He is unique—there are other saviors, too. They deny His resurrection, or spiritualize it. They emphasize His role as a "great teacher." They certainly will have nothing to say about the Blood of Jesus washing away our sins.[2] No matter how ethical or moral the teaching may be, no matter how loving and beautiful and attractive, no matter how logical, if it does not present Jesus as the divine Son of God become flesh, dying on the cross and shedding His Blood for the forgiveness of sins, rising again physically from the dead, you may be sure that you are dealing with a false cult. If you find much emphasis on the teachings of Jesus, but little on His Person, you may be sure you are dealing with a false cult.

Christianity is not founded on the *teachings* of Jesus, but on the Person of Jesus. It isn't what He taught, but Who He is, that matters most. To quote a popular proverb: "It isn't *what* you know, but *whom* you know, that makes the difference"! Also, if Jesus is

---

[2] The cults will sometimes talk about the "Blood of Jesus," but not as a remedy for sin. They will pick up such phrases as "power in the Blood," but to them it means an occult power that can *do* things for them.

The "power of the Blood of Jesus" is not a generalized spiritual "power," but the power to wash away sin. Since the cults do not usually believe in sin, they are not likely to be interested in this!

hailed as just a "great teacher," what can we do with His own claims to be God, and the Son of God? [3] If His claim is false, He is either not telling the truth, or He is mistaken . . . neither would be in keeping with the role of a "great teacher"!

Usually a cult centers around a strong leader, for whom often is claimed a supernatural authority and power. Sometimes this leader is asserted to be a "messiah" or "avatar of the divine," and sometimes to be literally and personally "god."

Many of the cults draw ideas directly from the pagan religions— Buddhism, and Hinduism, for example. We have mentioned reincarnation, which is in the very fiber of these religions, but there is also the idea of "pantheism"—that God *is* everything: the creation *is* God. God is the good and the bad, the high and the low, the male and the female, love and hate, life and death, the rose and the rattlesnake.[4] There can be no real differentiation between good and evil, for God not only creates both, they say, but He *is* both. The "fulfillment" for these religions is not a personal fulfillment in God, but an utter loss of the person into the "all," or into the nothingness of "Nirvana." [5]

[3] For example: Mark 14:61–64; John 5:18, 23, 26, 39; 6:33–35, 38, 46–51; 8:58; 20:28–29.

[4] The devil delights in confusion. In general whenever you have a confusion of thinking or definition, you should suspect that the enemy is at work somewhere. Where light is called darkness, up is called down, male confused with female, etc., you may well suspect that you are dealing with false doctrine. For example, some of the cults speak of the "father-mother god." Several of the false teachers today are saying that Adam, the original human being, was both male and female, and that these two aspects became separated. This usually goes on into a doctrine of "soul mating": everyone has a male or female somewhere who is his or her "other half." This kind of thinking opens the door wide to all kinds of abuses, tragedies, and perversities.

[5] Jesus' command that a man should "deny himself" has often been identified with this Hindu-Buddhist concept of self-loss. The whole content of the Holy Scripture is against this interpretation. The Scriptures tell us that God desires us to have fellowship and communion with Him, to be His children, to enjoy Him, even to be His *friends*. All this must meàn not loss of identity, but a heightening of identity in Christ. The oriental religions solve the

These pagan religions themselves have been experiencing a revival, not only in the Orient, but in the United States. Even the militant faith of Mohammed is being adopted, in a somewhat modified form, by the adherents of some of the "militant" groups.

Some people who are not involved in any particular cult will tell you that they are interested in "metaphysics," and that they are "seekers after truth." Metaphysics is that branch of philosophy which is man's attempt to reach into the unknown. It is understandable that a person who has not yet met God would want to use his inquiring mind to speculate about what's "out there," but this kind of speculation often leads the person directly into some cultic or strange teaching. The metaphysician confuses the soul and the spirit, thinking that the spiritual is an aspect of the psychological, and that the spirit is really the "deep unconscious," or something of that sort.[6] "Canst thou by searching find out God?" ask the Scriptures, and the answer is "No, not by intellectual and philosophical searching can you find God." You can

---

problem of the self by getting rid of it; they solve the problem of life by getting out of it. Christianity directs us to get rid of the *false* self, the "old man," in order that our true nature, the new creature in Christ, can come to fulfillment.

[6] Even men of undoubtedly orthodox belief get into trouble when they try to be "metaphysical" and appeal to the so-called intellectual. The beforementioned identification of the soul with the conscious mind, and the spirit with the "unconscious" or "subliminal" mind, is a good example of this. This identification is quite false, and yet it appeals to the metaphysician, because he desires to make everything understandable and accountable to the intellect, so that all must ultimately be some aspect of "mind," and thus controllable by man's mind and will. Typically, the metaphysically minded person, confronted by God answering prayer, or healing the sick, will say:

"This is taking place in obedience to a 'higher law.'" The implication of this is that some day *man* will understand and use that "higher law." Christian healing and answered prayer is not the result of obedience to an imagined "higher law," but the work of a sovereign and omnipotent God, Who is subject to no law except His own. All so-called law is simply a description of the way God chooses to do things, in accord with His own Nature.

only seek God by your "heart," that is, by your inner hunger to meet Him, the personal God, not a set of abstract principles. People say: "I'm seeking the truth," but Jesus says: "*I* am the Truth!"

Metaphysics, the attempt of the *mind* to come into contact with God directly, instead of through the spirit, may easily lead a person into the most dangerous area of all, the area of the psychic or occult. When Satan moved in and took over this world after the fall of man, he created a counterfeit spiritual realm, and any human being who tries to find God, or to come into contact with God, or to influence God, by his own psychological efforts, by thinking, willing, or feeling, is likely to come into contact with Satan's "spiritual" world which is more accurately termed the "psychic" world. Today, psychic and occult ideas and practices are flooding the scene, and being accepted by untold thousands of people, many of whom are "good members" of churches. In fact those very people who are the most determined to "find out" about God, in this way are the very ones most likely to be victimized.

We may sum up the "occult" or "psychic" beliefs as follows:

1. *Precognition* or *"fortune-telling."* The idea that a human being can validly foretell the future by means of visions, crystal balls, playing cards, palm reading, ouija boards,[7] meditations,

---

[7] We feel led to give special "dishonorable mention" to the ouija board. This little gadget is a polished board with the alphabet imprinted on it, and numbers from one to ten, with the words "yes" and "no." Over this board slides a little heart-shaped piece of wood, with a felt backing, called a "planchette." The person or persons using the board place their hands on the planchette, and it moves to spell out messages by indicating the letters of the alphabet. Again, this device is treated like a game, but it is not a game. It works, and can bring the users under deep bondage and oppression of the enemy. Sadly, it is sold every year by the millions as a game for children. If you have a ouija board in your home, burn it immediately, claim the protection of the Blood of Jesus, and ask the Holy Spirit to drive out whatever evil has been let in by the use of the board. Be very careful where and what your children are involved in when they visit other homes.

drugs, etc. Lurking behind this concept of "precognition" is the idea of a fixed "fate," an unchanging future that is already laid out and cannot be changed. This is in itself a totally unscriptural notion. Christians don't believe in "fate" or "destiny," but in a living God, Who guides all things. God is "the Eternal"—meaning the "ageless" or timeless—outside of time. Time is His *creation*. God knows the future, not because He *foresees* it, but because He *sees* it; He is already *there*, just as He is in the present and the past. He gave His Name to Moses as "I AM." The future is dependent on the free actions of free beings, and of God. If Satan is able to deceive people into thinking they can know the future, he can also make them believe that "what will be, will be," and adopt a fatalistic attitude toward life. The strange contradiction is that actually people want to know the future in order to try to change it; yet if the future were a fixed "fate," it would be useless to try to change or avoid it!

Fortune-telling or precognition is often confused with Biblical *prophecy*. One of the most popular fortune-tellers of our day, a woman whose life is the subject of a best-selling book, has been consulted for guidance by high government officials. Her skill with a crystal ball and the other paraphernalia of fortune-telling has made headlines, and she is hailed even by some presumably Christian leaders as a "prophet in the Old Testament tradition," in spite of the obviously occult nature of her activities. The fact is

---

Many young people's and even children's parties these days involve some kind of occult or psychic game or activity. Many a "slumber party" ends up as an amateur seance, or with the ouija board being brought out. We have heard of cases where teachers encourage their students to bring a ouija board to class with them and use it. We have even heard of cases where a Sunday-school teacher did the same thing! Explain these things to your children, so that they will be intelligently warned. Remember that their best protection, of course, is that they have met the Lord Jesus and accepted Him as their own Savior, and have received the baptism in the Holy Spirit. Until they have received the Holy Spirit, most Christians are unaware of the danger of such things, which makes your task more awkward, but God will give you wisdom.

that fortune-telling is strongly condemned and forbidden in the Bible (Deut. 18:10–13). Biblical prophecy is not *foretelling*, but *forthtelling*. The fortune-teller says: "I have the power to peer into the future, and I will tell you what I see!" The Biblical prophet says: "I was talking to God, and *He* told me to tell you . . . !" If a prophet of God foretells the future, he does so because God has chosen to share with him something that He, God, is going to do. There is usually a condition: "If you don't do such-and-such, I will do such-and-such." The scriptural prophet claims no special powers of precognition; he claims that God has spoken to him.

2. *Extrasensory perception: telepathy, clairvoyance, etc. Telepathy* or *mind reading* is the idea that a human being can detect and read the thoughts of another person, or can project his own thoughts to another person.

Not long ago, in Montreal, Canada, Dennis chatted with a young lady who was very active in Christian work—a "fundamental" believer.

"I'm studying telepathy," she said, a little defiantly. "Why do you say it's wrong? There's nothing about it in the Bible!"

"You mean you're learning to read minds?" he inquired.

She nodded her head.

"Tell me," he said. "After you have learned to read minds, how long will your marriage last?" She looked startled, and he followed his advantage: "How many friends will you have, when they know you can read their minds?"

"I see what you mean," she said slowly.

Telepathy or mind reading is one of the psychic practices that is forbidden by God. Nothing could more quickly destroy human community and fellowship than the supposed ability to read another person's thoughts.

Clairvoyance is the idea that a human being can obtain information from beyond his physical senses by "occult" or psychic means.

As we mentioned above, clairvoyance has gained a good deal

of publicity lately through the rise of a new cult that centers around the life and doings of a famous clairvoyant. This man claimed to be able to diagnose diseases and prescribe cures by means of his occult powers.

So-called water witching, or dowsing, must be included in this category. This refers to the use of a forked stick, or similar device, that allegedly bends down to indicate the presence of water, or of other things. (There is a report that men in the armed forces overseas are being taught the technique of "dowsing" for the location of land mines!) Those who do this are rarely trying to engage in psychic or occult practices, but think of it as the utilizing of some obscure "scientific" principle, e.g., "rays." It is, however, a subtle form of clairvoyance, and like other psychic practices, will bring oppression to the people who do it. Some well-diggers or drillers will not work on a "witched" well, experience having taught them that trouble usually follows when water is located in this way. The very nickname "water witching" shows recognition of the true nature of this practice.

Another popular parlor game, that is really clairvoyance, is the "pendulum," in which an object on a string or chain is hung over a person's hand, and questions are asked. The swinging of the pendulum allegedly indicates the answers. This could also be categorized a fortune-telling device. It should be let alone, and if you have engaged in any such practice, pray to renounce it, and cast out any spirit of oppression associated with it.

Satan, our spiritual enemy, would love to have us try to learn to do these things. Actually, it is likely that there is no such power, but that all so-called extrasensory perception (ESP) is the direct action of the powers of darkness—Satan and his angels and demons—bringing the information to the person who is foolish enough to seek it. If you attempt to read someone's mind, or to foresee the future, or to gain information from a distance by clairvoyance, Satan is overjoyed. He has access to the information that you are seeking, and he can bring it to your mind, knowing that you will think that you have acquired the power to do it yourself. This way he accomplishes several things: (a) He causes you to become more proud and self-centered, and even though you may be "doing good" with your supposed abilities, you yourself are becoming more and more self-important; (b) He is setting you, and all who are believing you, up for a mighty letdown. In Shakespeare's *Macbeth,* Banquo says, referring to Macbeth's experience with the three witches:

" 'Tis strange, yet oftentimes the instruments of darkness tell us truths. Win us with honest trifles, to betray us in the deepest consequence!" [8]

3 *Astrology.* The belief that the stars, planets, sun, and moon have a mysterious influence over human beings, establishing their personalities and characteristics, and affecting the events of their lives. The advertising market today is flooded with "astrological" gobbledygook. One soda-pop company is actually offering "computerized" horoscopes! The popular singers croon about the "Age of Aquarius." Young people are encouraged to select their wives or husbands by their astrological sign, and there are actual cases of marriages breaking up and the parties marrying other people whose horoscopes are more favorable! Many people regard astrology as a kind of game, and read their daily horoscope "just for fun." It is far from a laughing matter, however, for astrology is really a carefully concealed form of idol worship—what the Bible calls the "worship of the hosts of heaven." It ascribes personality and power to the heavenly bodies, often under the very names of the ancient gods and goddesses who were and are themselves fallen angels who have been working for the destruction of mankind for millennia. You can read your horoscope day after day and treat it as a joke, but the day will come when it will get your attention by coming true, or working out, causing you to take it a little more seriously. It will not be long—if you are as unfortunate as many have been—before you are reduced to al-

[8] *Macbeth,* Act I, scene 3.

most total dependence on the little column in the paper, being terrified to leave the house until the daily newspaper arrives! Leave astrology *alone!*

The Bible says that God put the stars and the other celestial bodies in the sky for "signs," and sometimes this will be quoted to you as an excuse for believing in astrology. But astrology does not claim that these things are just "signs"—which they are— but that they have power to influence human lives.[9]

4. *Techniques of so-called mind expansion* by *drugs, hypnotism, transcendental meditation*, etc. The idea here is that the mind can be opened to receive a wider understanding of the nature of things by these methods. What actually happens is that the mind is rendered passive and vulnerable to the enemy, who is only too glad to provide pretty lights while he is taking the opportunity to implant his own evil influences. It is no coincidence that the so-called hippie culture, based on drug use, is directly associated with occult practices of all kinds, and is also associated with many kinds of degrading and degenerate activity, especially sexual promiscuity and perversity. Satan loves to

---

[9] Do not confuse astrology with astronomy. Astronomy is the scientific study of the heavens, naming and identifying objects in outer space, and trying to understand their nature.

Another confusion arises from the fact that the Bible clearly says that God put these objects in the heavens for "signs" (Gen. 1:14). It is not wrong, therefore, to believe that God may use unusual activity or manifestations in the heavens to convey a message to man. The Wise Men who came to visit the Child Jesus were not necessarily astrologers. They were "Magi," the nearest thing to scientists in that day. They detected from their study of the heavens that God was about to perform some great Action upon the earth. This is *not* astrology. The Star of Bethlehem did not *cause* the birth of the Savior, nor have any influence on His life. It was a *sign* only. Daniel the Prophet was considered by the Persians to be a "Mage," or Wise Man (Dan. 2:10–13; 5:11). We have no indication, however, that he practiced astrology.

Notice that the Bible is saying that God may, for His purposes, cause there to be a *correlation* between events in the heavens and events upon the earth. Astrology is erroneously saying that the activity in the heavens *influences* and *causes* the events upon the earth.

mock and ridicule mankind, and surely nothing could be more of a mockery of the beauty and fittingness of man as God made him, or woman as God made her, than the ridiculous outfit of the typical "hippie"—the effort on the part of the male to look grotesque, and often effeminate; the similar attempt on the part of the girls to appear ugly, bedraggled, and dirty; the confusion of the sexes in dress and behavior.

Hypnotism is particularly dangerous, because it is thought of as a valid form of therapy in psychology and psychiatry, or as an alternative to anesthesia in medicine and dentistry. The fact is that hypnotism, too, by placing the soul in a passively receptive state, even when the hypnotist has no such intention, opens the door to morbid spiritual influences that may bring oppression that lasts for years, until the person is delivered through prayer and exorcism.

At a recent conference, a Christian leader who works with disturbed young people told of dealing with a teen-age girl, the daughter of a Methodist minister, who had been hypnotized, at the age of eleven, at a Christmas program in her father's church. This was just a "for fun" thing—an amateur hypnotist at a party —and certainly no harm was intended. The girl, however, behaved abnormally from that point. Her whole personality changed; her parents were unable to reach her. She became involved in some serious misbehavior, including car theft. At the age of fourteen, she was ministered to for deliverance, and was set free from the spirit that had moved into her personality when she innocently submitted to hypnotism.

Do not allow yourself to be hypnotized for any reason whatsoever.

5. *Sorcery* or *witchcraft*. In one sense, everything we are talking about in this part of the book is a form of sorcery or witchcraft, for we may define sorcery or witchcraft (also called "magic") as the effort to gain power and control in the "spiritual" world so as to get information, influence other people, get wealth

and power, or other material advantages. Much so-called religion is really *magic*. If the main purpose in your "religion" is to learn to *control* God, your religion is really a form of "white magic," even if it is good things you are seeking for yourself and others. The purpose of the believer is to get to know and love God. Fortunately for us, God desires to bless us in every way, and therefore we find, as we get to know Him, that He wants us to ask and claim good things for ourselves and others. He delights to give them, as we believe for them, but He Himself is always the greatest Good and the greatest Gift. "Seek first the Kingdom (Kingship) of God, and His righteousness, and all these things shall be added to you . . ." (Matt. 6:33).

In the narrower sense, *sorcery* and *witchcraft* comprise such things as "hexing," or influencing or harassing others by psychic and occult means. The newsstands are now blossoming out in an evil cluster of books on how to hex your enemies. Even "witchcraft do-it-yourself kits" are being sold, with complete instructions on how to make a wax doll to stick pins into!

6. *Certain physical phenomena: telekinesis, levitation, astral projection. Telekinesis* is the attempt to control the movement of matter by thought, e.g., the throw of dice, or the fall of cards. *Levitation* is the attempt to neutralize gravity by psychic means, so as to lift objects off the ground, tip tables, or raise oneself from the ground. *Astral projection* is the attempt to project the so-called "astral body" to a distance by psychic means. These things actually can happen, and the power behind them is demonic.

7. *Spiritism or spiritualism.*[10] This is the attempt of human beings to get into contact with the "spirit world," and especially with their departed relatives and friends, through the help of "spirit

[10] *Spiritism* is the general name for the practice of attempting to contact the departed. *Spiritualism* generally is used of the *religion* built around this belief. *Spiritualists* have "churches," and often claim to be Christian. *Spiritists*, however, are sometimes atheists—believing in the existence of the "spirit world," but not in God. The Bible term for *Spiritism* is "necromancy," or "having familiar spirits."

guides" and mediums. This is the cruelest of all Satan's deceptions, and the one that is peculiarly abominable to God. Human spirits do not remain in this world after death, but are either with God in His Kingdom, or are in Hell awaiting judgment. The person who seeks to get in touch with a dead friend or relative by spiritualism, if he or she contacts a genuine medium, will be put in touch, not with the human spirit of that relative or friend, but with a demonic spirit masquerading as the human person. The details of dress, physical appearance, and other information, are available to the enemy. A person will say: "But I know it must have been my grandfather, for he spoke of things that only he and I knew about. He called me by a pet name that only he and I used. . . ." But Satan and his helpers know about these things. Spiritualism may make its way into the life of Christian believers in very subtle ways. Many sincere Christians think it permissible to address the faithful departed in heaven, asking their prayer and/or intervention. Some claim departed saints appear and communicate with the living on earth. There is only one biblical example of a dead person returning as spirit to the earth, and that is Samuel (I Samuel 28), although many maintain that Samuel did *not* return, but that it was a demon masquerading as Samuel. The Scripture seems to state that it is Samuel, yet we do not feel that a doctrine

---

The Bible speaks of the Prophet Elijah coming back before the end. Does this contradict what we are saying? No. Elijah did not die, but is still in the body (II Kings 2:11). Nor is there problem over a person who died but has been revived (like Lazarus) for he or she is still in the body. Nor is there any problem with resurrected persons, like those who came out of their graves when Jesus rose from the dead (Matt. 27:52-3).

Jesus' transfiguration is cited by some as a return of two departed persons to the earth, Moses and Elijah. Elijah presents no problem, since he was not "departed," as we have said, but the Bible is clear that Moses died, although under unusual circumstances (Deut. 34:5-6, Jude 9). We believe however, if you read carefully you will see that the appearance of these two was not a *visitation*, but a *vision*. A visitation means that the person is actually present and communicating with those who see him or her. In a vision, the things seen are objective and real, but not physically present. The persons in a vision do not talk directly to those seeing them, nor invite themselves to be addressed. The Scriptures say that Moses and Elijah "appeared in glory" (Luke 9:31). They were "in glory," in heavenly places with Jesus, while their appearance was manifested on the earth. The vision faded immediately as Peter spoke, and afterwards Jesus said, "Tell the *vision* to no man, until . . . (Matt. 17:9). We believe the disciples had a glimpse of Jesus in heavenly glory, and in heavenly company.

The Roman Catholic Church teaches that Mary, the blessed Mother of Jesus, was taken to heaven without dying (the Assumption), as Elijah was, therefore, in terms of Roman Catholic doctrine, there is nothing unscriptural in the idea that Mary might appear upon the earth. We do not mean to say we can find scriptural evidence that she has done so, but to note that what we are teaching is not contrary to Roman Catholic doctrine at this point.

should be built on one reference. We accept the concept of "two or three witnesses" to confirm a teaching (Matt. 18:16, II Cor. 13:1). Nevertheless, even though you may believe Samuel's spirit returned, you still could not take this as precedent for communication with the departed, since it was one of the most serious offenses Saul committed. God permitted Samuel to appear (if it was Samuel) precisely in order to rebuke Saul's wrongdoing.

The term "communion of saints" in the Apostle's Creed has been misinterpreted by some to mean we can converse with departed saints. The "communion of saints" means all believers are members of Christ and of one another. In Jesus we are in communion with the faithful in heaven, but not in direct communication. It's good to keep the faithful departed in remembrance but we must wait until we get there, to sit down and talk with them! The closest we may come to communication is to say to Jesus "Please tell my mother I love her! Please tell such-and-such a person we love them and haven't forgotten them."

This detailed warning about the psychic and occult is desperately needed today, because the world is being flooded with this kind of thing. Serious-minded but misguided scientists are investigating these phenomena. One leading scientific laboratory has been investigating telepathy as a serious means of communication for years. Word now comes that Russian scientists have been studying these psychic "powers" with the purpose of using them in espionage. In almost all our colleges and universities throughout the nation there are classes in "parapsychology," which are studying such things as psychic phenomena, hauntings, witchcraft, reincarnation, etc.

People often say, and perhaps you may be saying at this point: "But in this and other books about the work of the Holy Spirit we are reading of wonderful Spiritual gifts and experiences, and now you seem to be telling us that they are wrong!"

No, we are telling you that there are two kinds of experiences, those that come from God, and those that the devil sends as counterfeits, and that it is of the utmost importance for you to be able to tell the difference! The great difficulty today is to distinguish the work of God from the work of Satan. The problem is that many do not believe in spiritual evil at all, but think that anything that seems "spiritual" must naturally be "good." This is why we have such a flood of weird doings. Our only safe guide is the Word of God illuminated by the Holy Spirit (Matt. 24:24; II Cor. 11:14).

We have made what may seem to some a long digression, but it is of great importance. Even though you yourself may not have been involved with any of the cults or the false teachings listed above, or others like them, you will be praying and counseling with other people, so we repeat this solemn warning: Do not encourage anyone to pray to receive the Holy Spirit unless you are sure that, first, he has received Jesus as his Savior; and, second, that he has renounced any involvement or relationship with any of the wrong beliefs or teachings listed in this chapter. These wrong beliefs carry with them demonic power, and if a person prays to receive "the Spirit," if he is not a Christian, and not indwelt by the Holy Spirit, or if he is a Christian, but has permitted a spirit of error to enter his mind, that wrong spirit may be the one expressed, and the wrong spirit may gain a deeper hold on his mind and body, instead of the Holy Spirit. The result can be spiritual and psychological confusion that may take years to overcome. The Apostle Paul had good reason to command: "Lay hands suddenly on no man!" It is incautious praying with people for the baptism in the Holy Spirit that leads to strange manifestations, that brings discredit to the work of the Lord, and sometimes drives seekers away.

What to do? As specifically as possible, if you have been in any way involved in these false cults or teachings, renounce them in the Name of Jesus. Ask God to forgive you; bind and cast out any spirit connected with the wrong teaching. Claim the protection of the Blood of Jesus, and ask the Holy Spirit to fill every area where any false beliefs have been.[13]

---

[13] Several cases have come to our attention in recent years of people with psychic and occult ability trying to bring these abilities to God to be used for Him. The desire is understandable, but God doesn't need Satan's secondhand goods! If you have such "powers," you must get rid of them, renounce them and cast them away from you completely, and let God give

Here is a prayer for you to use:

"Dear Father, if I have believed, studied, or practiced anything that is displeasing to You, or contrary to Your Word, I am truly sorry. I ask You to forgive me for being involved in these things, and I promise You that I will not have anything more to do with them, and if I have any books or equipment connected with them, I promise You that I will burn them right away.

"I renounce (here name the cult or false teaching) in the Name of Jesus Christ. Spirit of (here name again the cult of false teaching), I bind you under the Blood of Jesus Christ, and cast you into outer darkness, never to return, in Jesus' Name! Thank You, Jesus!"

Repeat this second paragraph for each cult or false teaching with which you have been involved.

After you have prayed to renounce and cast out these things, immediately pray, or have someone pray with you, that you may be filled with the Holy Spirit in every area where the false teachings have been. If you have not yet received the baptism in the Holy Spirit, proceed immediately to accept the full work of the Holy Spirit in your life, as described in the next chapter.

If you have any doubt about what we have been saying in this chapter, or if you do not agree with what we have said, *do not pray to receive the Holy Spirit* until you have received further counsel, and can accept freely what has been told here. You will find it helpful to read such books as, *The Kingdom of the Cults* by Walter Martin, *Angels of Light?* by Hobart Freeman, *Spiritual Warfare* by Michael Harper, *The Challenging Counterfeit* by Raphael Gasson.[14] The first three books deal with a number of the better-known cults; the last one deals specifically with spiritualism and spiritism.

---

you His gifts. Nothing but confusion can follow the attempt to bring these demonic practices into the service of the Lord.

[14] W. R. Martin, *The Kingdom of the Cults* (Minneapolis: Bethany, 1965). Hobart Freeman, *Angels of Light?* (Plainfield, N.J.: Logos, 1969). Raphael Gasson, *The Challenging Counterfeit* (Plainfield, N.J.: Logos, 1966). Michael Harper, *Spiritual Warfare* (Plainfield, N.J.: Logos, 1970).

5

How to Receive the Baptism
in the Holy Spirit

You have received Jesus as your Savior, you have renounced any false teachings that might hold you back or confuse you, and now you're ready to pray to be baptized in the Holy Spirit. Who is going to baptize you in the Holy Spirit? *Jesus* is going to do it! This being so, you can receive the Holy Spirit anywhere, anytime, can you not?

"But I thought someone had to lay hands on me to 'give' me the the Holy Spirit." No, we have already settled that. Because you have received Jesus, you already have the Holy Spirit, so no one needs to "give" Him to you, even if they could! Jesus is living in you, and He is ready to baptize you in the Holy Spirit as soon as you are ready to respond. Having someone lay hands on you may be a help, and it is certainly scriptural, but not absolutely necessary. We have already shown that on three occasions in the Acts of the Apostles, hands were imposed, but in two other cases they were not. Many people have received the Holy Spirit in recent years without anyone being near them except Jesus! You can receive the baptism with the Holy Spirit in church, at the altar rail, sitting or kneeling in the pew, driving your car down the freeway, vacuuming the rug, doing the dishes, or mowing the lawn. It will happen the moment you ask and believe.

"But do I have to speak in tongues?"

When Dennis was seeking to receive the Holy Spirit, he said:

"I'm not interested in this 'tongues' thing you are talking about!" He thought speaking in tongues was some kind of wild emotionalism, and his English upbringing caused him to be very wary of such things! [1] The Episcopalians who had been telling him about their experience laughed.

"Oh," they said. "All we can tell you is that it came with the package—just like in the Bible!"

We have shown that speaking in tongues is indeed a common denominator in examples of the baptism in the Holy Spirit given in the Scriptures. It seems obvious also that the early believers had a way of telling immediately whether or not their converts had received the Holy Spirit. Some say that we are supposed to tell when a person has received the Holy Spirit by the change in his life—by the "fruit of the Spirit." We certainly should be more "fruitful" Christians after receiving the baptism with the Holy Spirit, but "bearing fruit" is not the scriptural *sign* of this experience. The apostles knew right on the spot when a person had received the baptism with the Holy Spirit. If they had had to wait until they observed fruit or change of character in the person's life, it would have taken months and years to evaluate. Apparently the early Christians had a simpler way, and it isn't hard to see what it was.

What was it that drew the great crowd of "Jews, devout men, from every country under heaven" on Pentecost, three thousand of whom were converted that very day and hour? They weren't there long enough to find out what kind of lives the people were living before and after! What was it that immediately convinced Simon Magus that his neighbors had received something that would be so highly salable that he tried to purchase it? On the other hand, how did the apostles Peter and John know immediately that

---

[1] Dennis Bennett, *Nine O'Clock in the Morning* (Plainfield, N.J.: Logos, 1970), p. 18.

Philip's converts had not received the Holy Spirit? It certainly wasn't a lack of joy, for the record says: "There was much joy in that city" (Acts 8:8 RSV). What was it that completely convinced Peter at the house of Cornelius that the Romans had received the Holy Spirit, so that he dared, contrary to all previous practice or belief, to baptize these Gentiles? The case of the Ephesians we cited in Acts 19 is a little different, for these people had not received Jesus. Paul undoubtedly missed the presence of the Holy Spirit in them at all; but after they had received Jesus and been baptized in water, what was it that let Paul know, right after he had laid his hand on them, that they had received the Holy Spirit?

"We do hear them speak in our tongues the wonderful works of God" (Acts 2:11 KJV). "They heard them speak with tongues and magnify God" (Acts 10:46 KJV). "They spoke with tongues and prophesied" (Acts 19:6 RSV).

Anyone who takes the Scriptures seriously can scarcely avoid coming to the conclusion that speaking in tongues is important. Jesus Himself said: "These signs shall follow them that believe, they shall speak in new languages" (Mark 16:17).[2]

---

[2] We are quite aware that this passage at the end of Mark has been questioned by scholars, and put down by many as a "later addition." In some popular modern translations it has been "demoted" to a footnote at the bottom of the page. A friend of ours, Mr. George Gillies, a capable leader in small-group ministry, says of this: "Even in a footnote, it still *works!*"

It doesn't take any great scholarship to see that there is a break between the 8th and 9th verses of Mark 16—but whoever supplied the "lost ending" of the Gospel of Mark, whether it was Mark himself or someone else, it came from the earliest period, and was accepted in the early days of the Church. It became a part of the canonical Scripture. While this "lost ending" is missing from the two earliest extant documents we have, it is present in many others. Everything in it is confirmed elsewhere by other incidents of Scripture. We say of this passage: "It may have been a 'lost ending,' but somebody found it and stuck it back in our Bible! Apparently the Holy Spirit wanted it there!" We must be very careful about following the teaching and textual criticism of those scholars of the liberal-modernist tradition, who would like to "desupernaturalize" the Scripture as much as possible.

The Apostle Paul said plainly to the Corinthians:
"I want you all to speak in tongues!" (I Cor. 14:5 RSV).
The Greek original here:

$$\Theta \acute{\epsilon} \lambda \omega \ \delta \grave{\epsilon} \ \pi \acute{\alpha} \nu \tau \alpha \varsigma \ \acute{\upsilon} \mu \tilde{\alpha} \varsigma \ \lambda \alpha \lambda \epsilon \tilde{\iota} \nu \ \gamma \lambda \acute{\omega} \sigma \sigma \alpha \iota \varsigma$$

"Thelo de pantas humas lalein glossais," can be translated either as simple present indicative, or in the subjunctive—the form is the same. Most English translations, including the King James Version, choose the subjunctive: from "I would that ye all spake with tongues" all the way to the farfetched "I might wish that you all spoke with strange sounds" of *Good News for Modern Man!* The reason is easy to see. The translators of these versions presumably did not know what speaking in tongues might be, and therefore did not feel easy in adopting the most straightforward translation of Paul's words. The Revised Standard Version, however, has no such hesitation, but selects the present indicative as the most likely translation: "I want you all to speak in tongues." The literal translation of Bagster's *Englishman's Greek New Testament* is also direct: "Now I desire you all to speak with tongues."

After all, it is the same Apostle Paul who says later to the Corinthians: "I thank my God I speak in tongues more than any of you!" or, as it may be perhaps more accurately translated:

"I thank my God, speaking in tongues, more than any of you" (I Cor. 14:18).

Paul goes on to say: ". . . if I pray in a tongue, my spirit prays, but my understanding is unfruitful. What is it then? I will pray with the spirit, and I will pray with the understanding also: I will sing with the spirit, and I will sing with the understanding also" (I Cor. 14:14–15).

And here we have an answer to what speaking in tongues is, and why God should have chosen such a seemingly strange evidence to accompany the baptism with the Holy Spirit. Speaking in tongues is prayer *with* or *in* the Spirit: it is our spirit speaking to God, inspired by the Holy Spirit. It takes place when a Christian believer speaks to God, but instead of speaking in a language that he knows with his intellect, he just speaks, in childlike faith, and trusts God to provide the form of the words. The regenerated human spirit, which is joined to the Holy Spirit, is praying directly to the Father, in Christ, without having to accept the limitations of the intellect. As the new life in the Spirit is expressed, or exercised, if you like, the spiritual life is built up or edified.

"He that speaks in a tongue edifies himself" (I Cor. 14:4). "Edifies" is the translation of the Greek word *oikodoméo* which means quite literally to "build up." Here it means to build oneself spiritually. A related word is used by the Apostle Jude when he says: "Building yourselves up on your most holy faith, praying in the Holy Spirit" (Jude 20). (Quite clearly in this passage Jude is referring to speaking in tongues.) The intellect, on the other hand, not understanding the language is humbled; the soul (psychological being) is put in its place, which is subject to the spirit. Prayer is said to God in freedom. The prayer comes just as the Holy Spirit intends it to come; therefore it is a perfect prayer, from the perfectness of the new creature, and perfectly inspired by the Spirit.[3] Therefore it is also *effective* prayer. The Father can receive it wholly, for it comes not from our still-messed-up souls, but from the Holy Spirit through our spirit, offered by our volition and cooperation.

[3] A fascinating proof of this is that people who are totally deaf, and have never spoken a word, when receiving the Holy Spirit will speak fluently in tongues! Mrs. Wendell Mason of LaVerne, California, who works with the deaf, says: "I have seen and prayed with at least twenty deaf persons to receive the Holy Spirit, and heard them begin to speak fluently in a heavenly language to God, then return to their sign language when communicating with me. I have seen two deaf-mute persons receive the Holy Spirit and speak in tongues." Similar testimony comes from many others who work with the deaf. It would be absolutely impossible for these handicapped people to imitate a language, or to be speaking words remembered from their "unconscious" mind (as some skeptics have said in trying to explain away speaking in tongues) since they have never heard a word in their lives!

Our voice, our speech, or as the Bible calls it, our *tongue,* is our chief means of expression, and it is no coincidence that it is here that the Holy Spirit chooses to flow out first. Spiritually, psychologically, and physiologically, our ability to speak is central. In Proverbs we read: "A man's belly shall be satisfied with the fruit of his mouth; and with the increase of his lips shall he be filled. Death and life are in the power of the tongue: and they that love it shall eat the fruit thereof" (Prov. 18: 20–21 KJV). Our ability to communicate with one another in rational speech is a fundamental part of being human. The King James Bible speaks of the faculty of speech as the "glory" of the body. The Psalmist says:

"Awake up, my glory; awake, psaltery and harp: I myself will awake early" (Ps. 57:8 KJV). And in another place: "Therefore my heart is glad, and my glory rejoiceth: my flesh also shall rest in hope" (Ps. 16:9 KJV). In each case the margin explains that "glory" is a metaphor for the *voice.*

In the third chapter of James, he compares the tongue to the rudder of a big ship, able to control the whole vessel with very little movement, or to the bit in the mouth of a horse, a small object that controls the whole animal. However, James goes on to say that the tongue is an "unruly evil, full of deadly poison" (Jas. 3:8 KJV). He says that the tongue, being set on fire with the fire of hell, can defile the whole body (Jas. 3:6). Psalm 12:4 (KJV) says: "With our tongue will we prevail; our lips are our own: who is lord over us?" It would seem that the same faculty of speech which is so great a thing, is also the main thing that obstructs the freedom of the Holy Spirit in the believer's life. It is a focus of our intellectual pride. A neurosurgeon friend made this interesting comment one day: "I understand why God uses speaking in tongues. The speech centers dominate the brain. I don't see how God Himself could do much about the physical brain unless He got hold of the speech centers!"

"Who can tame the tongue?" asks James, and the answer is: "The Holy Spirit!" and speaking in tongues is the main part of the process. The Spirit says: "I want to inspire and rule the most important means of expression you have—the ability to speak. I also want to tame and purify that with which you *sin* the most, your tongue!"

Speaking in tongues has nothing to do with emotion! Speaking in tongues *cannot* be emotion, for the emotions are part of the soul, the psychological nature, while speaking in tongues is speaking from or in the spirit (I Cor. 14:14). This fact may surprise people who have heard a highly emotional manifestation which was actually a misuse of the *gift* of tongues (public ministry in tongues) and perhaps have been frightened or repelled by it.

The passages in several modern versions of the Scripture that speak of "tongues of ecstasy," or "ecstatic speech," are paraphrases rather than translations. There is nothing in the Greek original to imply that speaking in tongues had anything to do with excitement, ecstasy, frenzy, etc. The phrase is always just *lalein glossais*, meaning simply, "to speak in languages." Speaking in tongues may stir the emotions, just as it may sharpen the intellect, and order the will, and we hope it does these things; but you do not have to become emotional in order to speak in tongues. As a matter of fact one of the greatest blocks to the receiving of the Holy Spirit is the highly charged emotional atmosphere that is thought by some to be helpful or even necessary. When people are seeking to receive the baptism in the Holy Spirit and speak in tongues for the first time, we try to keep their emotions as "calm" as possible. Many begin to speak in tongues rather quietly. Later they will speak more strongly as faith grows and fear is overcome. Actually, excited emotions get in the way of the Holy Spirit just as much as an overactive intellect or an overdetermined will!

There is nothing wrong with *emotion*. We need to learn to express and enjoy our emotions much more than we do, especially in regard to our fellowship with God. What could be more wonderful, or more emotionally stirring, than feeling the presence of

God? Emotion, however, is a *response*, an expression, not a *cause*. *Emotionalism* is the expression of emotion for its own sake, without any roots or reason.

You will not be in some "strange" frame of mind when you speak in tongues. It has no relationship with the weird, the occult, the "way-out," as we hope we have made very clear to you in the last chapter. It isn't hysteria or any form of suggestion. You don't go into a trance, or make your mind a blank. When you are speaking in tongues your mind should be actively thinking about the Lord! Blankness or passivity of mind are dangerous things in any circumstances, and should not be encouraged.

There is no *compulsion* involved in speaking in tongues. God does not *compel* His people to do things, He *inspires* them. It is the enemy who "possesses" and compels people against their will. Whenever anyone says: "I do this because God *makes* me do it!" referring to any physical manifestation, it is likely that it is not God at all, but either his own soulish (psychological) nature that is acting, or worse yet, an alien spirit that is oppressing him.[4] God

[4] We are not denying that the Holy Spirit can sovereignly cause physical sensations. It is not uncommon for a person to feel a supernatural movement upon cheeks, lips, or tongue, or a stammering tongue, or trembling of the body, when praying for the baptism of the Holy Spirit, and this can happen even to a person who is not only not actively desiring to pray for the receiving of the Holy Spirit, but who perhaps does not understand the matter. There are cases of people experiencing a weakness of muscles, even to the point of not being able to stand up! On the day of Pentecost itself they were accused of drunkenness! At Caesarea the Romans were overwhelmed by the Holy Ghost seemingly without expecting such a thing to happen. Certainly Peter had not mentioned any such manifestation, and did not expect it to take place! Nonetheless, no matter how overwhelming the inspiration may be, and whether it is spiritual, psychological, or even physical in nature, the spirit of the prophet is still subject to the prophet. The consent and cooperation of the individual is always required. No matter how powerful the inspiration, it is never *compulsion*. Notice, however, that the Spirit can and does compel *unbelievers*. Those who came out to arrest Jesus were thrown to the ground. Paul was knocked down and temporarily blinded. One can think of many other examples.

can and does do unexpected and unusual things, but does not make His children behave in bizarre and grotesque ways that would frighten others (II Tim. 1:7).

In the same vein, many are afraid to speak in tongues because they think they may pop up in church and interrupt the preacher, or suddenly speak in tongues on the golf course! Nonsense! The "spirit of the prophet is subject to the prophet" (I Cor. 14:32). Some say: "But if this is the Holy Spirit speaking, how can I dare to refuse Him?" Ah, but you see this *isn't* the Holy Spirit speaking. Speaking in tongues is *your* spirit speaking, *inspired* by the Holy Spirit, and your spirit is under your control. Your consent is always needed before you manifest any gift of the Spirit. Sometimes you may be so strongly inspired by the joy and power of the Lord that you *want* very much to speak out in a situation where your mind tells you it would be wrong. That's all right to feel that way; you learn to control yourself just as you learn not to laugh at the wrong time, even though something strikes you as very funny, and you are much inspired to laugh! Indeed, this is a good comparison, for the inspiration of the Holy Spirit is much like joyful laughter.

"I thought the Bible said that there must be no speaking in tongues without interpretation?" This rule applies to speaking in tongues in a public meeting, and will be discussed in more detail in a later chapter on the *gift* of tongues, but here we will only say that private speaking in tongues needs no interpretation. The believer is "speaking to God in a mystery," praying with his spirit, not his intellect.

"What if I don't speak in tongues? Can I receive the Holy Spirit without speaking in tongues?"

"It comes with the package!" Speaking in tongues is not the baptism in the Holy Spirit, but it is what happens when and as you are baptized in the Spirit, and it becomes an important resource to help you continue, as Paul says, to "be being (or keep on being) filled with the Holy Spirit" (Eph. 5:18). You *don't* have to speak in tongues in order to be saved. You *don't* have to speak in tongues in order to have the Holy Spirit in you. You *don't* have to speak in tongues to have times of feeling filled with the Holy Spirit, but if you want the free and full outpouring that is the baptism in the Holy Spirit, you must expect it to happen as in the Scripture, and to do what Peter, James, John, Paul, Mary, Mary Magdalen, Barnabas, and all the rest did! If you want to understand the New Testament you need the same experience that all its writers had. A man said to Dennis one day:

"I would like to receive the Holy Spirit, but after a *Wesleyan* manner!"

Dennis' answer was: "There's only one way to receive the Holy Spirit, and that's in a *New Testament* manner!" (John Wesley would certainly have agreed!)

People will say: "But what about the great Christians of history? They didn't speak in tongues!" Are you sure? There is probably not a time in church history when there were not some who knew the fullness of the Holy Spirit and spoke in tongues. Whenever there has been a strong revival of the faith, the gifts of the Spirit have made their appearance. St. Patrick of Ireland, St. Francis of Assisi, St. Teresa of Avila, St. Francis Xavier, probably Martin Luther, the early Quakers, the Waldensians, the early Methodists are a few examples of those in earlier days who spoke in tongues. In more recent times the great Charles Finney did. It seems very likely that D. L. Moody did.[5] Many Christian leaders today speak in tongues but do not admit to it because they fear prejudice. Yet there are many who are more bold. There are thousands of ministers and priests in virtually all the denominations who testify that they have received the baptism in the Holy Spirit and spoken in tongues, and the number is growing all the time. An organization of charismatic Presbyterian ministers alone numbers around four hundred. Five years

[5] Carl Brumback *What Meaneth This?* (Gospel Publishing House, 1949) chap. 6.

ago, an American Baptist leader told us that there were at that time five hundred American Baptist ministers who had received the Holy Spirit and spoken in tongues.

There are a number of people who have spoken in tongues, but don't know it! Every now and then when talking about this manifestation someone will say: "Oh, you mean that funny little language I have spoken ever since I was a child—is *that* it? It makes me feel happy and close to God!" [6]

A pleasant little Dutch lady, perhaps thirty-five years of age, was talking with Dennis after a meeting recently.

"I spoke in tongues once, about eight months ago," she said, a bit wistfully, "and I'd like to do it again!"

"Why don't you?"

"Oh, I wouldn't dare to try. You see, I have a little play language that I talk for my children when we're having fun together. They think it's funny, and we have a good time. I'm afraid that if I tried to speak in tongues, that little play language would come!"

By this time Dennis was smiling: "That's your tongue!" he said.

The little lady was startled: "Oh no," she said, shaking her head firmly, "that's just a play language!"

After several more minutes of discussion, Dennis said to her:

"Would you be willing to speak this little 'play language' as you call it, to God? Talk to God in it?"

It took a little more persuasion, but finally she bowed her head and began to talk quietly in a beautiful language. In not more than thirty seconds, she was in joyful tears: "That's it! That's it!" she said.

A young couple from England who were touring the United States stopped at St. Luke's some seven years ago. They were curious to find out more about the baptism in the Holy Spirit.

[6] Obviously, for such a thing to be valid, the child would have had to receive Jesus Christ first.

As they talked, we tried to explain to them what speaking in tongues meant. A half-amused, half-puzzled smile came on the face of the young man:

"Could this be something I've been doing in my prayers ever since I was three years old?" he asked. His wife also smiled: "Me, too!" she said. Unknown to one another, they had both been speaking in tongues from time to time in their prayers ever since they were very young children.

Perhaps this is a good time to mention that quite often people first speak in tongues in their dreams! The week before writing this chapter, we spent some time with an airline's jet pilot who was seeking to find out more about the Holy Spirit. He said:

"The other night I dreamed I spoke in tongues. When I woke up, I felt so wonderful!" When a person speaks in tongues in his dreams he will soon begin to speak in tongues in his waking hours if he yields. It is hard sometimes to convince people of this! A young man from a nearby Lutheran school attended the St. Luke's Friday Night Information Meeting together with some other students. He came by the church the next week and said: "Oh, I was so disappointed. You know I wanted to stay and receive the Holy Spirit the other night, but the others had to go home. But that night I dreamed I came to the altar rail in your church and received the Holy Spirit. It was so great! I spoke in tongues, and was just overjoyed!"

"Hm-m-m," said Dennis. "The meeting was in the parish hall, wasn't it?"

"Yes," replied the young man. "I've never been in your church auditorium itself, but in my dream that's where I was!"

"Would you mind describing it to me?" Dennis asked.

"Well, I noticed that the altar itself was in an unusual position. It was so far out from the wall that I could have reached out and touched it as I knelt at the side of the altar rail." (This was about seven years ago, when freestanding altars were not so common.) "The church was painted brown—it was all wood—"

and the young man proceeded to give a pretty good description of the inside of St. Luke's Episcopal Church, Seattle! It seemed the Lord had not only baptized this man in the Holy Spirit in the dream, but had also given him a very recognizable picture of the inside of St. Luke's! (This last would have been a manifestation of the gift of knowledge.)

"Congratulations!" said Dennis. "You've received the Holy Spirit!"

"Oh, no," said the boy, "it was just a dream!"

It took a while to convince him, but at the end of that time, he consented to pray, and immediately began to speak fluently in a new language.

"That's the same one I spoke in my dream!" he said happily.

Before praying to receive the Holy Spirit, we suggest that you first pray to the Father in Jesus' Name, reaffirming your faith in Christ, thanking Him for the new life He has given you in Jesus, and for the Holy Spirit living in you. Continue praying, saying whatever you have on your heart. If you can remember anything that would keep you from coming closer to God, any unconfessed wrong action or wrong attitude, a grudge against someone, for example, or a dishonest deal in business, tell God about it, confess, and then promise Him that you'll straighten it out. If you feel so led, leave your prayer for a time, go and put the thing right, and then return (Matt. 5:23–24), but don't let any notion of some "hidden" or unknown sin keep you from claiming the baptism in the Holy Spirit. "I'm not worthy," some people say, and the answer is: "Of course you're not worthy!" Jesus alone is worthy, and He'll provide the worthiness. Would there ever be a time when you would come to the Lord and say: "Now I'm worthy. So please give me what I have coming to me!" Better not do that—you might get it!

If you are by yourself praying to receive the Holy Spirit, say this prayer, or if someone else is praying with you, they will say a similar prayer for you:

"Heavenly Father, I thank You that I am under the protection of the precious Blood of Jesus which has cleansed me from all sin. Dear Lord Jesus, please baptize me in the Holy Spirit, and let me praise God in a new language beyond the limitations of my intellect. Thank You, Lord; I believe that You're doing this right now! In Jesus' Name I pray."

When you ask Jesus to baptize you in the Spirit, you must receive. Receiving is something *you* do. Rita likes to speak of the "ABC's" of receiving:

A. *Ask* Jesus to baptize you in the Holy Spirit. The Book of James says: "You have not, because you ask not" (Jas. 4:2). God gave you a free will and never will take it away. He won't force His blessings upon you, as this is not the way of Love. You must ask.

B. *Believe* you receive the moment you ask. "Ask, and you *shall* receive that your joy may be full" (John 16:24). Faith is present-tense belief. "*Now* faith is . . ." says the writer of Hebrews (Heb. 11:1). Faith is also active and not passive, which means you must take the first step.

C. *Confess* with your lips. When you received Jesus as Savior, you believed in your heart and confessed Him with your lips. Now confess with your lips, but in the new language that the Lord is ready to give you. Open your mouth and show that you believe the Lord has baptized you in the Spirit by *beginning to speak*. Don't speak English, or any other language you know, for God can't guide you to speak in tongues if you are speaking in a language known to you. You can't speak two languages at once! Trust God to give you the words, just as Peter trusted Jesus to let him walk on the water. Speaking in tongues is a childlike act of faith. It involves no ability, but rather the setting aside of ability. It is simply speaking, using your voice, but instead of saying what your mind wants you to say, you trust the Holy Spirit to guide your voice directly to say what He wants you to say.

"But that would just be *me* speaking!" Exactly! *God* does not speak in tongues—*people* speak in tongues, as the Spirit gives the words. On the day of Pentecost we read: "They began to speak—in other languages—as the Spirit gave them utterance." So you must *begin to speak, in other languages*—not your own language or languages—as the Spirit gives the utterance, or the form of the words, to you—and He will! Just like a child learning to talk for the first time, open your mouth and speak out the first syllables and expressions that come to your lips. You must *begin to speak,* just as Peter had to get out of the boat. God will guide you when you dare to trust Him by stepping out in faith.

When praying to receive the Holy Spirit, people will sometimes experience such things as, involuntary trembling, stammering lips, or chattering teeth. These are physical reactions to the Holy Spirit that are in themselves without meaning, except that they may indicate His presence. They probably arise out of our resistance to Him. Some have waited for years for the "stammering lips" to become a language, but in vain. The believer must always begin to speak—speaking in tongues is *not* involuntary.

"But I don't want to be told how to speak in tongues! I want *God* to do it! Otherwise it might be 'in the flesh'!"

No one can possibly tell you "how to" speak in tongues! All we are trying to do is to get you to begin to do it! It is true that many people begin to speak quite spontaneously without any urging at all. In the Bible apparently most of them did. If we were all living in simple faith, we would do so too, but unfortunately many of us tend to be sophisticated and inhibited, fearful of simpleness. Today still, many adults and children with childlike faith receive easily and often spontaneously; mainly our instruction here is for those who have "hang-ups" at this point. All we are saying to you is that it is up to you to get out of the boat if you want to walk on the water. We can't tell you *how* to walk on the water, Jesus will take care of that, but we can urge you to get out of the ship—to take the first step on top of the waves! As far as "in the flesh" is concerned, a leading Bible teacher says:

"When Peter got out and walked on the water, the 'flesh' were all sitting in the boat!"

The "flesh" is the opposite of faith—it is the "old man," rebellious and sinful. It is far more "fleshly" to wait for God to take you over, and *make* you do something, than to trust Him in simple faith to honor you as you begin to utter sounds of speech. You may have fear about speaking out in this way because you were taught that speaking in tongues was a sign of the baptism in the Holy Spirit, but that most people did not speak in tongues again except under a "special anointing," that only certain privileged persons were enabled to pray in tongues whenever they chose, because they had received the "Gift of Tongues." Thus, if a person made a few sounds, someone might say: "Praise God, he's got the Baptism!" and let it go at that! If it were true that most believers only prayed in tongues once, at the time of receiving the Holy Spirit, and perhaps never again, or very rarely, it would be of paramount importance to be sure that those first "utterances" were totally inspired by the Spirit, and not human effort. We are teaching, however, what we know to be true, that these first efforts at obeying the Spirit are only the beginning. It doesn't matter if the first sounds are just "priming the pump," for the real flow will assuredly come.

The Psalmist said, by the inspiration of the Holy Spirit:

"Open your mouth wide, and I will fill it!" (Ps. 81:10) and, "Make a joyful noise unto the Lord!" (Ps. 81:1).

A joyful noise may not yet be speaking in tongues, but even this is pleasing to the Lord. It won't be long before it will be your Holy Spirit language, as God will honor your simple faith.

Several things may happen at this point: you may not succeed in beginning to speak, due to self-consciousness and inhibition. That's all right—you haven't "flunked" the test! You simply have to keep on until you do decide to make that first sound. It is like the parachutist jumping out of the airplane for the first time. If he wants to be a parachute jumper, he's got to jump! There's no other way! Don't back off at this point as some do, and say:

"I guess God doesn't want me to have it!" It's you who are holding back!

You may begin to speak, but only get out a few halting sounds. That's wonderful! You've broken the "sound barrier"! Keep on with those sounds. Offer them to God. Tell Jesus you love Him in those "joyful noises"! As you do, they will develop and grow into a fully developed language. It may take days, or even weeks —not because of God, but again, because of you. In a very real sense, any sound you make, offering your tongue to God in simple faith, may be the beginning of speaking in tongues. We have seen lives visibly changed by the release of the Spirit brought through one sound—one little syllable! If you have ever uttered one such sound while trusting God the Holy Spirit to guide you, from then on don't say: "I haven't spoken in tongues yet," but rather: "I'm beginning to speak in tongues!" Remember the manifestations of the Spirit are always God and us working together. "The Lord working with them . . . with signs following" (Mark 16:20 KJV).

Then again you may begin to speak immediately in a beautiful language. That's wonderful, too, but it doesn't mean you're any holier than the others! It just means that you are a little freer in your spirit, and less inhibited. In any case, the thing to do is to keep on speaking—or keep on trying to speak.

Now and then a person will have some new words in his mind before he begins to speak in tongues. Speak them out! Others will follow.

Occasionally someone will see words written down, as if on "ticker tape," or as if projected on the wall. One woman saw the words in her "tongue," as if they had been written on the wall, complete with pronunciation and accent marks! She "read" them as she saw them, and began to speak in tongues! Why should such things happen? Because the Holy Spirit enjoys variety! Most people don't get these little "helps," so if you do, just praise the Lord. Some are more able to sing than to speak, and that is fine. You can just as well begin by singing in the Spirit as by speaking in the Spirit! Just allow the Spirit to give you the tune as well as the words. At first it will probably come as a little chant, perhaps on one or two tones, but it may help you to get free. We know people who can't sing a note "in the natural," but who sing beautifully in the Spirit!

What am I supposed to *feel* when I speak in tongues? At first, you may feel nothing at all. Remember, this is not an emotional experience. You are trying to let your spirit have freedom to praise God as the Holy Spirit inspires. It may be a little while before your spirit can begin to break through to your feelings, giving you a new awareness of God within you. On the other hand, you may experience a sudden breakthrough and feel as if you were carried right up into the heavenlies! Praise the Lord! It's wonderful to do that—to become suddenly aware of the fullness of Christ in you, and be carried up by it. Many people just sense a lightness and reality down in their spirit as they begin to speak, and the awareness grows.

One thing is sure, though: if you don't accept the experience as real, you won't be aware of its reality! The Christian life is built on faith—trust and acceptance. Inevitably many will say: "That was just me!" Of course it was you—who did you expect it would be, somebody else? It was you speaking, while the Holy Spirit provided the words! But until you accept that it is the Holy Spirit, and that the experience is real, you are obviously not going to get the blessing you are looking for! So believe and accept, and praise the Lord for what He is doing in you and through you!

One day Dennis was asked to give his testimony at a nearby church. After the meeting many stayed to pray to receive the Holy Spirit. The pastor said to Dennis:

"There is a pastor here who is having a difficult time. Can you help him?" It was a young minister from one of the very stiff liturgical churches. He was determined to receive the Holy Spirit, but obviously very far out of his element in this rather uninhibited setting! The more the well-meaning pray-ers exhorted him, the more he froze!

Dennis asked him to come to his office at St. Luke's, and there, after some reassurance, they quietly prayed that he would receive the fullness he was seeking. After a short time, he began to tremble violently, and then to speak beautifully in a new language. He continued to speak for perhaps two or three minutes, then stopped, looked at Dennis rather glumly, and said:

"Well, thank you very much," and took his leave!

The next evening he telephoned:

"Dennis," he said, very sadly, "I'm really grateful to you for trying to help me, but you know, I didn't receive anything!"

Dennis was on the verge of saying: "Too bad. Better luck next time!" when the Lord's wisdom showed him how foolish that would have been. Instead he said:

"Look here, my friend! I saw you tremble under the power of the Holy Spirit, and I heard you speak beautifully in a language you do not know! I know you know the Lord Jesus as your Savior, so I know this must have been the Holy Spirit! Stop doubting! Start thanking the Lord for baptizing you in the Holy Spirit!"

The man hung up, but he called back in about an hour. He was "riding high"! "Oh," he said, "when you told me to do that, I began to thank the Lord for baptizing me in the Spirit, and, wow! The joy of the Lord hit me, and I'm really on cloud nine!" It wasn't long before we heard that revival was starting in his little church!

If you have just come through a period of great strain or grief, in which you have been required to keep a firm hold on yourself and your emotions, you may have difficulty in letting go to permit the Lord Jesus to baptize you in the Spirit. You have been hanging on, and you are afraid that if you let go, you will really "go to pieces." It is very likely, if this is your circumstance, that as you attempt to release your voice to the Lord, you may begin to weep. Go ahead and weep! The Holy Spirit knows just how to untie those knots! Sometimes people will weep when they receive the Holy Spirit, sometimes they will laugh! We prayed with a young Episcopal priest and his wife some eight years ago, and as they received the Spirit, the young man roared with laughter, while the wife wept copiously, and both were filled with the joy of the Lord! Our Lord knows what you need, and He will meet you in the way that is the most helpful to you.

There are some believers who have asked to be baptized in the Holy Spirit, but have been unable to begin to speak in tongues. They consider this to be because God doesn't want them to do so; it isn't for them. We find, however, that with proper explanation, and answering of questions, and instruction, such persons often will break through their inhibitions and begin to speak in the Spirit.

With others we find, after counseling with them, that they have been involved in the past with cults, or occult practices—as explained in detail in chapter four. They have discontinued these practices, but have never *renounced* them. After being led to renounce them, they begin to speak in tongues right away.

We are convinced, from the Scriptures and after praying with thousands of people to receive the baptism in the Holy Spirit over the past ten years and more, that there is no believer who cannot speak in tongues, if he or she is properly prepared, and really ready to trust the Lord.

After Jesus has baptized you in the Holy Spirit, your life will begin to have real power. It's like a soldier getting ammunition for his rifle, and consequently Satan, the enemy, will not be pleased. Many Christians do not believe there is a real enemy, a personal devil; that's why they spend their lives sitting in his prisoner-of-war camp! The moment you receive the fullness of the Holy Spirit, that is, the minute you begin to allow the power of God to overflow from your spirit into your soul and body, and into the world around, Satan becomes painfully aware of you, and you will begin to be aware of his work. He will give his attention to "shutting you down" if possible.

Jesus' ministry of miracles and power did not begin until after He had received the power of the Holy Spirit, and immediately following this He was tempted by Satan in the wilderness (Matt. 3:14-17; 4:1-10). Our new lives in the Spirit are patterned after Jesus.[7] When we receive the power of the Holy Spirit, we will also be put to the test. Because Jesus was victorious, we too will be!

The Book of James says: "Submit yourselves therefore to God. Resist the Devil, and he will flee from you."

"Submit yourselves therefore to God" means that the first and most important defense is to stay in fellowship with God; keep on praising Him, enjoying His presence, actively believing and trusting Him. Don't let anything quench your new freedom in fellowship with the Lord.

[7] Some say: "That's right! And Jesus didn't speak in tongues when He was empowered by the Holy Spirit, so why should we?" It is true that Jesus did not speak in tongues, but He said that we would do so. Jesus did not need the edification of speaking in tongues, and there were no barriers in His soul that made it necessary for His Spirit to speak to the Father in a language His mind did not understand. Indeed it is impossible to imagine Him doing so. Moreover speaking in tongues is the manifestation that was to come at Pentecost, in "the fullness of time." We have already seen that it was when Jesus went back to be with His Father in Heaven, that the Holy Ghost could then be given in His fullness, which in turn made speaking in tongues possible. Jesus had said: "The things that I do, you will also do, and you will do greater things, because I am going to My Father." (John 14:12) The ability to speak in languages we have never learned, then, could be seen as part of the "greater things" that Jesus said we would do after He had gone back to Heaven.

The next thing is: "Resist the devil and he will flee from you" (Jas. 4:7 KJV). Jesus' way of resisting was to use the Scriptures: "It is written . . . it is written." The Scripture is the Sword of the Spirit. Find some swordlike Scriptures and memorize them so that they will always be with you.

"Behold, I give unto you power . . . over all the power of the enemy: and nothing shall by any means hurt you" (Luke 10:19 KJV).

"Greater is he (Jesus) that is in you, than he (the enemy) that is in the world "(I John 4:4 KJV).

"For the weapons of our warfare are not carnal, but mighty through God to the pulling down of strong holds" (II Cor. 10:4 KJV).

You will be wanting to tell others what has happened to you, but be sure to wait until the Holy Spirit directs you. Not everyone will be ready for your witness when you think they should be, so share only as the Holy Spirit opens the doors. Prepare yourself to be an effective witness by seriously studying the Scriptures mentioned in this book.

When a person receives the baptism with the Holy Spirit it doesn't mean he's "arrived" spiritually, as we're sure you understand having read this far. Don't ever yield to the enemy's temptation to cause you to feel superior; pray for the fruit of humility; it is a good antidote. The baptism with the Holy Spirit is just the *beginning* of a new dimension of your Christian life, and it is still up to you whether you will grow or regress. If you continue to choose to put the Lord first in your life, then you are on the road to glorious adventures in our Lord Jesus Christ!

6

Introduction to the Gifts of the Holy Spirit

If you have been baptized in the Holy Spirit, you are now becoming more aware of the gifts of the Spirit. Two words are used commonly in speaking of the gifts: one is *charisma* (or plural, *charismata*), gift of God's love; the other is *phanerosis*, manifestation.

The simple word "gift" is a good word, as it serves to remind us that these blessings cannot be earned but that they are freely given by God to His children. A gift is not a reward for good behavior, but a sign of relationship. You give your children birthday presents because they are your children, not because they have been "good." The word "manifestation" means a showing forth, a making visible, or making known. This word shows the gifts of the Spirit to be the ministry of Jesus shown through His people today. The words, "gifts" and "manifestations" together, give us a fuller picture of the work of the Holy Spirit.

We, the members of the body of Christ, should believe that God will show His love through us as needs present themselves day by day. When a person needs healing we should expect God to manifest the gift of healing through us to the needy person. The gifts aren't owned by us. The person *ministered* to receives the gift. We should not claim to have any certain gifts, but let us remember that Jesus, the Gift of God, lives in us, and within Him are all good gifts.

There have been two extreme ideas about manifesting the gifts of the Holy Spirit in the Church. The most prevalent has been that God permanently gives a particular gift or several gifts to certain individuals and they therefore become, for example, the official "speakers in tongues," "interpreters," or "healers." In support of this way of thinking some may quote the Scripture which says: "To one is given by the Spirit the word of wisdom; to another the word of knowledge by the same Spirit . . ." (I Cor. 12:8 KJV) and so forth, not seeing that this chapter is speaking of a church meeting where the Holy Spirit is inspiring one person and then another to manifest various gifts. It doesn't mean that one individual is given one or more permanent gifts. This mistake—claiming to have permanent gifts—leads to pride, to stagnation, and tends to limit God's other gifts in that person. Another result is a focusing down on a few people to express the gifts while the majority of the congregation sit by as spectators with no expectation that God may want to work through them.

The other extreme has been the idea that *everyone* baptized in the Holy Spirit has all nine gifts of the Spirit to manifest whenever *he* chooses, sort of an independent "one man band"! While it is true that the gifts reside within Christ in us, yet the Scripture clearly teaches that they are manifested only at the Holy Spirit's discretion (I Cor. 12:11). God is trying to show us that we need one another, that we can't get along all by ourselves. The body of Christ is made up of *many members*, and God has purposely planned the release of the gifts "as He wills" so that Christians would need one another in order to function effectively for Him. We must "discern the Lord's body," by looking for Christ in other Christians or we will greatly hinder and limit what God desires to do.[1] We should be praying for God's glory to be shown in the lives of others as well as in ourselves.

[1] This does not mean that we should condone what others are doing when they are openly proclaiming false doctrine (Eph. 5:11), but minor differences should not be allowed to break our fellowship.

It is true, however, that as Christians mature, certain gifts may be expressed more frequently and effectively through them. It is then said that they have a *ministry* in those gifts. The person with such a ministry should encourage those who are new to enter into the gifts also and should be careful himself, not to get so focused in his particular ministry that he stops expecting God to work through him in other ways. God is a God of variety!

As two Christians were talking one day one said: "Well you can *have* the gifts, I'll take the *fruit!*" [2] The gifts of the Holy Spirit are various ways in which the power of God works through the life of the believer. The fruit of the Holy Spirit is the character and nature of Jesus Christ being shown in the life of the believer. Jesus didn't only say to the sick who came to Him: "I love you," but He said, "Be healed!" One of the saddest things to experience is loving people and not being able to help them! Both the fruit and the gifts are vitally important. To date, however, there has been much more teaching and encouragement about the fruit of the Spirit in Christendom than about the gifts[3] of the Spirit.

The Holy Spirit inspired Paul to admonish us to learn about the spiritual gifts: "Now concerning spiritual *gifts* brethren, I would not have you ignorant" (I Cor. 12:1). In this book we will define each gift, give New Testament examples in the life of Christ and others, some references to Old Testament usage, and what we may expect for the Church today. It will show how seven gifts were manifested in the Old Testament and Gospels from time to time as people were moved upon by the Holy Spirit.

These seven are:

1. The "Word of Wisdom."

---

[2] The fruit of the Spirit, according to Galatians 5:22–23 is "love, joy, peace, patience, gentleness, kindness, faith, humility, discipline."

[3] I Cor. 12:8–10: "the word of wisdom, the word of knowledge, discerning of spirits, gift of faith, working of miracles, gifts of healing, prophecy, various kinds of tongues, interpretation of tongues."

2. The "Word of Knowledge."
3. The Gift of Faith.
4. The Gifts of Healings.
5. The Working of Miracles.
6. The Gift of Prophecy.
7. The Discerning of Spirits.

It will not require too much thought on the reader's part to remember incidents in the Old Testament and Gospels where these were manifested.

To these seven were added two more since the Day of Pentecost.

8. The Gift of Tongues.
9. The Interpretation of Tongues.

thus making up the total of nine Gifts as listed by the Apostle Paul in I Corinthians 12. Thus believers who have not yet experienced Pentecost may manifest any of these seven gifts occasionally, much of the time not even recognizing them as such. However, after the fullness and overflow of the Spirit, any or all nine gifts may be manifested frequently and in power through the life of the believer.

Do not confuse the first seven Gifts listed above with the "Seven-Fold Gifts of Grace" mentioned many places in Christian literature and liturgy—for example, in the Confirmation rite of several of our denominations, or in the widely known Latin hymn: *Veni Creator Spiritus*:

> "The sevenfold gifts of grace are thine,
> O Finger of the Hand Divine!" [4]

This refers to Isaiah 11:2, which says, speaking of the coming Messiah: "And the spirit of the Lord shall rest upon him, the spirit of wisdom and understanding, the spirit of counsel and might, the spirit of knowledge, and of the fear of the Lord." You will see that these are not Spiritual gifts at all, but characteristics

[4] *Book of Common Prayer,* p. 544.

of the Holy Spirit in His sevenfold Nature, referred to in Revelation 1:4 as the "seven spirits" which are before God's Throne, the sevenfold Spirit of God. Nevertheless, we can see a direct relationship between these last six characteristics of the Holy Spirit (the first one being "The Spirit of the Lord" Himself), and the ninefold Gifts.

Those who are willing to be used in the gifts of the Holy Spirit must learn to listen to God. Too much of the time we do all the talking. The beginner is bound to make some mistakes. A child learning arithmetic is not expected to learn without making errors! Rest assured that even mistakes will be turned to God's glory as we trust and rely completely on Him.

"Every good gift and every perfect gift is from above, and comes down from the Father . . ." says James (Jas. 1:17). It is obvious that God's gifts are perfect, but we need to be reminded that the mortal channels through whom they are expressed are not. Just because a person manifests the gifts does not mean that he is walking closely with the Lord. As the word "gift" implies, the gifts are not earned or retained—even by living a good life. The Book of Romans tells us: "The gifts and calling of God are without repentance" (Rom. 11:29 KJV). Don't follow a person just because he has a "gift ministry." Instead, look for the fruit in his life, for honesty and purity brought about by the Spirit of Truth—the *Holy* Spirit—and a hunger for and appreciation of God's Word. Look for balanced teaching between literal and spiritual meanings of the Scripture, look for fellowship with other brethren; and then receive only that which is quickened to you by the Holy Spirit, and which agrees with the Scripture. Remember, *Christians don't follow signs, signs follow Christians.*

The gifts of God, when expressed as the Lord intended them to be, are beautiful, and needful in order that the body of Christ may grow and develop. They are not merely to be tolerated, but are greatly to be desired. We should be forewarned against two mistakes frequently made in the past: misuse of the gifts by a lack of scriptural order, and rejecting or quenching the gifts of the Spirit. The second mistake is often a reaction against the first one.

In Christ you have been given all good things freely (Rom. 8:32); however, the promises of God must be appropriated by faith. The gifts will be manifested according to your faith: "According to your faith be it unto you" (Matt. 9:29 KJV; Rom. 12:6). Let us manifest His gifts in faith, love, and obedience, that God's people may be strengthened and prepared for their difficult but glorious tasks ahead.

We are not going to study the Gifts in the same order they are presented in I Corinthians 12, but will group them into three classes, as follows:

A. Inspirational or Fellowship Gifts. (The power to *say*.)
   1. The Gift of Tongues.
   2. The Gift of Interpretation.
   3. The Gift of Prophecy.
B. Gifts of Power. (The power to *do*.)
   4. Gifts of Healings.
   5. The Working of Miracles.
   6. The Gift of Faith.
C. Gifts of Revelation. (The power to *know*.)
   7. Discerning of Spirits.
   8. The "Word of Knowledge."
   9. The "Word of Wisdom."

The order in which the Gifts are listed here has no reference to their relative importance, any more than it does in the Scripture itself, but it will help us to see the relationship of the manifestations with one another.

7

The Gifts of Tongues and Interpretation

The Gifts of utterance—tongues, interpretation, and prophecy—are not to guide our lives by, but to help unfold God to us, and to help us in our response to Him. They are to turn us God-ward and to give us a healthy fear (awe) of the Lord.

We will look at the gifts of tongues and interpretation together, since they should always be manifested together in a public meeting. Some have said that speaking in tongues and interpretation of tongues are the least of the gifts, because they are the last gifts listed in I Corinthians 12:7–11. If there were any special reason why these gifts are last in the list, a more logical one would be because they were given to the Church last! The first seven gifts in the list are found in the Old Testament and the Gospels, but these two were not given until Pentecost.

There are *two ways* speaking in tongues may be manifested. The most common is as a devotional language for private edification, needing no interpretation (I Cor. 14:2). This has already been discussed in detail. What we will be talking about now is the public manifestation of tongues, which should be interpreted. We will term *this* the "gift of tongues." When a baptized-in-the-Holy-Spirit Christian is inspired to speak in tongues aloud in the presence of others, with interpretation of tongues usually following, this is the *gift* of tongues (I Cor. 14:27–28; 12:10). The gift of tongues is delivered or given to the listeners, and they are edified by the gift of interpretation which follows.[1] It is preferable that tongues and interpretation should not be used in groups of unbelievers or even uninstructed believers, without an explanation of what they are—either before or after the manifestations.

There are two main ways the gift of tongues may be expressed in the gathered church:

1. Through the gift of tongues and interpretation God may be speaking to the unbeliever and/or to believers.

Although God, Himself, doesn't speak in tongues (how could there be a language unknown to Him?), yet, He does guide the yielded Christian to do so, and through tongues and interpretation does speak to His people today. Both the Old and New Testaments give joint witness that God does speak to His people through these gifts. Isaiah says:

"For with stammering lips and another tongue will he speak to this people" (Isa. 28:11 KJV). St. Paul quotes this as he explains speaking in tongues and interpretation: "It is written, 'With men of other tongues and other lips will I speak unto this people . . .'" (I Cor. 14:21 KJV), or the literal Greek translation reads: "In other tongues and in lips of others I will speak to this people . . " Also the Scripture implies that the gift of tongues plus interpretation is equal to prophecy, which is always God speaking to the people (I Cor. 14:5b).

The gift of tongues is not a sign to the believer since he doesn't need a sign, but it may be a sign to the unbeliever (usually unsought for), causing him to accept the Lord Jesus Christ. "Wherefore tongues are for a sign, not to them that believe, but to them that believe not . . ." (I Cor. 14:22 KJV).

How the gift of tongues can be a sign to the unbeliever:

a) The tongue may be a language known to the unbeliever with God speaking directly to him.

[1] The gift of tongues may also be prayer or praise to God.

b) The tongue may not be a known language, but the powerful impact of the message in tongues, normatively accompanied by interpretation, may speak to the unbeliever, and be a sign to him.

When tongues are a message from God, coming to the unbeliever either by his knowing the language (a translation), by the inspired interpretation through a believer, or in some rare cases even without benefit of interpretation or translation, they are a sign to the unbeliever that God is real, alive, and concerned about him.

In a Full Gospel church in Oregon, there was a young man who had married a Japanese girl while stationed in Japan with the armed forces. The young couple returned to the United States, and were doing well, except that the young lady flatly resisted her husband's Christian faith and held steadfastly to her Buddhism. One night, after the evening service, the couple was at the altar, he praying to God through Jesus Christ, and she praying her Buddhist prayers. Next to them was kneeling a middle-aged woman, a housewife from the community. As this woman began to pray out loud in tongues, suddenly the Japanese bride seized her husband's arm:

"Listen!" she whispered in excitement. "This woman speak to me in Japanese! She say to me: 'You have tried Buddha, and he does you no good; why don't you try Jesus Christ?' She does not speak to me in ordinary Japanese language, she speak temple Japanese, and use my whole Japanese name which no one in this country knows!" It is not surprising that the young lady became a Christian!

We have known of many similar cases. What actually happened in this situation is that as the American housewife was yielded to God in *praying in tongues*, the Holy Ghost chose to change the language from prayer *to* God—to a message *from* God—through the *gift* of tongues.

Ruth Lascelle (then Specter)[2] had been brought up in an Orthodox Jewish home. When in her early adult life, her mother accepted Jesus as her Messiah, Ruth thought her mother had lost her mind. She went to her mother's Full Gospel church to try to disprove their beliefs. At one meeting there was a message in tongues which, although uninterpreted, had such a great impact on Ruth that she knew in that moment that Jesus was real, and she too accepted Him as her Messiah.

Here is an example of the gift of tongues, although neither understood nor interpreted, yet being a sign of such strength that Ruth was converted on the spot. Ruth says: "I asked God to give me a sign to show if the Christian faith was really true. At the time of course, I had never heard of the New Testament Scripture: 'The Jews required a sign' " [3] (I Cor. 1:22 KJV).

Another interesting scene took place in 1964 in Northern California at a charismatic Episcopal church service. A college student had come to the meeting with her father, an important ecclesiastical official. This young lady had known Jesus in her childhood, but had gotten further and further away from Him during her college years. Her faith had been pretty much smashed and she was under psychiatric care. Near the close of the meeting the gifts of tongues and intepretation were manifested in love and with power. Tears began to pour down her face as she made her way to the altar for prayer. She told the person counseling with her:

"When I heard speaking in tongues for the first time tonight, and the message that followed, I knew once again without a doubt that God is real and He loves me!"

This last is an example of these gifts as a sign, not to an unbe-

[2] R. R. Specter, *The Bud and the Flower of Judaism* (Springfield, Mo.: Gospel Publishing House, 1955).
[3] An uninterpreted gift of tongues in a meeting is of course irregular, but in this case God used it.

liever, as previously recorded, but rather to a temporarily un-believing believer.

The gifts of tongues and interpretation may also be a message from God to bless and exhort faithful people. Examples are numerous; we will take time to give only one. One Friday night about a year after Rita was renewed in her experience of the baptism in the Holy Spirit she was attending a prayer meeting. She prayed for a friend who was working as a missionary nurse in Africa, and was having some difficult trials. As she finished praying for Dorothy, there was a gift of tongues and interpretation, which said in effect: "If you, yourself, are willing to go and help your friend, your prayer will be answered much more quickly." Then the Lord asked Rita three times, just as Peter had been asked: "Do you love Me?" She had been walking closely with Him, and had been an active witness for Him ever since her renewal; it was such a surprise to be asked if she loved Him, that she began to weep. Rita told God, then and there, that she loved Him so much that she was willing to go wherever He wanted her to go. So convincing was the message the Holy Spirit had given that at the end of the meeting her friends gathered around to bid her farewell! As it turned out, although she was willing to go to Africa, two months later the Lord sent her instead—to Texas!

2. The gift of tongues may also be public prayer to God.

Most of us would rather hear from heaven than from earth; we would rather hear God speak to us, than hear man speak to God. Yet in reading the Scripture, we see the gift of tongues used as prayer in a public meeting and needing interpretation so that other believers can be in agreement (I Cor. 14:13–16). Therefore, the gift of tongues plus interpretation may also be prayer, thanksgiving, or praise to God, which encourages the congregation. The gift of tongues as prayer or praise may be in a language known by unbelievers, as happened on the day of Pentecost: "We do hear them speak in our tongues the wonderful works of God." Paul also says that someone in the meeting may *sing* praise to God using the gift of tongues; the interpretation may also be given in song, which can be most inspiring.

Any baptized-in-the-Holy-Spirit believer can "sing in the Spirit." This means allowing the Holy Spirit not only to guide one's speech, but to sing as He guides the words *and* the tune. In a group of instructed believers a number of persons may pray or praise God, speaking or singing in tongues all together without interpretation being required. At times when an entire group joins in "singing in the Spirit," allowing the Holy Spirit not only to guide individual voices, but to blend them together, such harmony is produced that it sometimes sounds like the angelic choir itself! If singing in the Spirit or praying in the Spirit occurs in a large group, and all are not instructed believers, a scriptural explanation should be given by the leader as soon as possible. Many unbelievers have been touched by God in such situations—when the meeting was guided with wisdom and according to the scriptural pattern.

Some have been puzzled when a brief utterance in tongues is followed by a long response in English. There are several reasons for this. It may be that the language the Holy Spirit gave was more concise than the more elaborate language of the interpreter. Then too, the interpretation itself may have been followed by words in prophecy. A further explanation may be that the speaking in tongues was really private prayer, and the presumed interpretation actually prophecy.

Though all baptized-in-the-Holy-Spirit believers can and should speak in tongues daily in their prayers, not all will minister the gift of tongues in a public meeting (I Cor. 12:30). You will know that God is prompting you to manifest the gift of tongues when you have a definite quickening or witness of the Holy Spirit within. This doesn't mean that you have to do anything impulsively. Talk to the Lord quietly and tell Him if He wants to use you in this way to make an opportunity in the service for you to minister. Never interrupt when another person is speaking. As

David duPlessis says, "The Holy Spirit is a Gentleman!" Ask the Lord if this is the particular gift He wants for the group. When bringing any of the oral gifts of the Holy Spirit—tongues, interpretation, or prophecy—be sure to speak loudly enough to be heard by all, but don't be unnecessarily noisy or use an affected tone of voice. Either of the latter will frighten some people, and make them wonder about the validity of the gift. It will keep them from hearing what God desires to say to them. Speak with the utmost concern for the welfare of all, and in the love of God. If you believe that God wants you to manifest the gift of tongues, be prepared to pray also for the gift of interpretation in case there is no other person present yielded enough to do so (I Cor. 14:13).

The *interpretation of tongues* is bringing the meaning of what has been said through the gift of tongues at a public meeting. A person feels moved to speak or sing in tongues, and either he or another is given by the Holy Spirit the *meaning* of what has been said. He or she cannot *understand* the tongue. It is not a *translation* but an *interpretation,* giving the general meaning of what was said. The gift of interpretation may come directly into the person's mind, *in toto,* or just a few beginning words may be given, and as the interpreter trusts the Lord and begins to speak, the rest of the message comes. In this way it resembles speaking in tongues—"You speak, the Lord gives the words." Interpretation may also come in pictures or symbols, or by an inspired thought, or the interpreter may hear the speaking in tongues, or part of it, as though the person were speaking directly in English. Interpretation will have the same result as a prophetic utterance, that of: "edification, exhortation, or comfort" (I Cor. 14:3–5). Remember, the gifts are not to guide your life by, but rather to confirm what God is already saying to you in your spirit and through the Scriptures.

God moves as He wills, but He does have a general pattern for us to follow. Some have called I Corinthians 14 the charismatic

Christian's *Robert's Rules of Order*. For example, I Corinthians 14:27 says, "If some speak in a . . . tongue, let the number be limited to two or at the most three, and each one [taking his] turn, and let one interpret and explain [what is said]" (Amplified Bible). This Scripture gives specific rules. It limits the number of utterances in tongues and interpretation to two or three times in any one meeting. Some think the next verse means that after two or three gifts of tongues an "official interpreter" should bring only one interpretation for the two or three utterances in tongues, but verse thirteen indicates that *anyone* who is used to manifest the gift of tongues may also pray to interpret. This is important to realize since others in the meeting may not be yielded enough at that moment to bring the needed interpretation. To keep from having tongues without interpretation causing confusion to unbelievers and uninstructed believers (v. 23, 33), it seems scriptural that each utterance in tongues should be interpreted singly. Also it would be difficult to retain an interpretation for any considerable length of time.

More speaking in tongues would no doubt be recognized as known languages if there were someone present who knew the language and could translate. It is also possible that some speakings in tongues are "languages of angels" (I Cor. 13:1). There are about three thousand languages and dialects in the world, so it is not surprising that few languages are recognized in any particular locality; indeed it is surprising that so many are. On the day of Pentecost there were about one hundred and twenty speaking in tongues, but only fourteen languages were recognized (Acts 1:15; 2:1,4,7–11), even though "devout Jews" were present from all over the then known world. This is about the percentage of known languages identified today. In praying with people for the blessing of Pentecost and being in numerous charismatic meetings in many parts of the world during the last ten years, we have known people to have spoken in tongues in Latin, Spanish, French, Hebrew,

Old Basque, Japanese, Aramaic, Mandarin Chinese, German, Indonesian, Chinese Foochow dialect, N. T. Greek, English (by a non-English speaker), and Polish.

At times those who have received the Pentecost experience are challenged by some who do not understand the purposes of speaking in tongues with such questions as:

"If you really have been given a new language, why don't you have it analyzed, find out what country it is from, and then go there as a missionary teaching the Gospel in that tongue?" Others challenge:

"If Pentecost is so great, how come missionaries with this experience still have to study language in school?"

These people don't realize that the gift of tongues is manifested to the unbeliever only as the Holy Spirit directs, and even though a person may be used once to speak a certain language, thereby reaching someone for Christ, he has no way of knowing that that specific language will ever be given to him again. Although a baptized-in-the-Holy-Spirit believer can speak in his private devotional tongue at will, yet in this and in the gift of tongues the choice of language he will speak cannot be regulated by the individual. God brings these vocal miracles to pass as He chooses and for His own purposes.

Then too some people mistakenly say the Gospel was proclaimed through the gift of tongues on the day of Pentecost and therefore this would be the only valid purpose for speaking in tongues today. This again is erroneous. Though some were heard speaking known languages by the power of the Holy Spirit on the day of Pentecost—yet they did not proclaim the Gospel in tongues but were instead heard praising God. The one who did the evangelizing that day was Peter. Though prior to his speaking to the people, he too had been edified by speaking in tongues, yet when he brought the message of salvation he spoke a language he understood, in a language all the listeners could understand.

There is a very common, but mistaken idea that the hearers on the Day of Pentecost were "foreigners" who did not understand the Aramaic dialect of Hebrew which was the common language and so had to have the Gospel presented to them in the languages of the countries from which they came. A more careful inspection of the record will correct this. The second chapter of Acts says:

"There were dwelling at Jerusalem *Jews*, devout men, from every nation under heaven" (Acts 2:5).

The people who heard the 120 first believers speaking in tongues on the Day of Pentecost were faithful Jews from the "Dispersion" or *diaspora*, which was the term used to describe the fact that already in those days the Jewish people were scattered all over the world. But just as they have done today, they kept their identity and brought their children up as good Jews. Even though they were born in foreign parts, and perhaps were brought up speaking another language, they were all taught the Hebrew tongue, and no doubt looked forward eagerly to the day when they would visit Jerusalem. The Day of Pentecost scene would be just as if English people from all over the world were to come to London for some great national event, say, the coronation of Queen Elizabeth II. Here are people from New Zealand, and Jamaica, and India—English in nationality, raised in English homes in faraway places, knowing and speaking the English language, yet never having seen "home." In their everyday lives they would often speak a "foreign" tongue. Imagine a group of such people coming to London for the coronation and suddenly hearing a group of cockney Londoners speaking beautifully in the language of the far-off countries from which they came!

"Are not all these which speak cockneys? How hear we then every man in the language of the country where we were born? . . ."

"Oh," say some, "you see they all *heard* in their own language. The disciples were speaking in a mysterious 'tongue' that miraculously sounded to each one like his own language." An interesting theory, but not scriptural! The Bible says: "They began to speak in *other languages* as the Spirit gave them utterance" (Acts 2:4).

When Peter addressed the crowd, he said to them:

"Men and *brethren* . . ." They were not foreigners, but "brethren," a term that the Jew did not use lightly! Besides, it is clear that when Peter stood up to tell them what was going on, he was not speaking in tongues. Fourteen nations and languages are mentioned—did Peter then speak in each of these fourteen languages in succession? Of course not; he spoke in a language which all understood. What would they have been doing in Jerusalem for the great feast day, if they were not able to understand what was going on? The record says that there were a few *proselytes*, that is, converts from the Gentiles, but these, too, would have been instructed in the Hebrew language.

Having made this general point that tongues are not normally used to proclaim the Gospel and were not used this way on the Day of Pentecost, let us also recognize, as always, there are exceptions to the rule. There are examples scattered through Christian history, of those who were given by the Holy Spirit the ability both to speak and understand a new language, this ability remaining with them. The great missionary to the Orient, Francis Xavier, according to his biographers, received the Chinese language in this way. Stanley Frodsham, in his book, *With Signs Following*, gives several similar examples in the modern Pentecostal movement.

John Sherrill, in the book, *They Speak With Other Tongues*,[4] tells of a missionary who in 1922 was used to bring the message of salvation to a tribe of cannibals through the gift of tongues. The missionary, H. B. Garlock, being captured and put on trial by the natives, spoke for some twenty minutes in what to him was an unknown language, but which the cannibals obviously understood and responded to by setting him free, and later turn-

---

[4] John L. Sherrill, *They Speak With Other Tongues* (New York: McGraw-Hill, 1964), pp. 107–111.

ing to Christ. It is significant that Garlock then returned to his own mission station, and continued ministering to Liberian people whose language he had no doubt taken much time and effort to learn. The cannibals' language was not given him permanently by the Spirit, but "loaned" to him for the emergency.

A young woman from St. Luke's Church, Seattle, some eight years ago stopped to talk with an unknown Asiatic woman while making a hospital call. The woman spoke very little English, but was able to say, in response to a gesture by the St. Luke's visitor indicating that she would like to pray with her: "I, Buddha! I, Buddha," meaning of course that she was a Buddhist. The girl from St. Luke's felt led to speak to the woman as the Spirit gave her the words, and for several minutes talked to the woman in a language unknown to the speaker. As the lady from St. Luke's took her leave, the other said, with a joyful face: "I! Jesus! I! Jesus!" Obviously the girl from St. Luke's had been witnessing to the Asiatic woman in her own language, and she had responded by receiving Jesus as her Savior!

Another unscriptural notion is that the Corinthians were the "Peck's Bad Boys" of the early Church! They did disorderly things like speaking in tongues, because they were only half-converted from their paganism! Paul had to lecture them on their emotionalism. He went along with them on their speaking in tongues but he didn't like it!

How wrong this is can be seen quickly, again, by really reading the New Testament. When Paul went to Corinth, God said to him: "I have much people in this city" (Acts 18:10 KJV). It was at Corinth that Paul met two of his greatest helpers, Aquila and Priscilla, and it was to Corinth that they brought Apollos, one of the most effective of the early evangelists. There is no implication that the Corinthians were in any way a second-rate bunch! Indeed, it is a popular misconception—that a great church is a church without problems. Just the opposite is true—the greater and stronger the work, the more problems Satan will try to stir up. The Corinthians had troubles because God was doing a great work among them, and it was being challenged by the enemy.

Paul did not remonstrate with the Corinthians because they were speaking in tongues, he did so because they were letting pride and party spirit come into their group. His great concern was their divisions—their sectarianism, which in turn led to a misuse of the gifts. Far from trying to get them to stop using the gifts, he urges them repeatedly: "covet the gifts," "earnestly desire them" (I Cor. 12:31; 14:1); "I want you to come behind in no gift" . . . "I want you to be enriched in all knowledge and all utterance . . . " he says to them; but also, "Let all things be done decently and in order" (I Cor. 1:7, 5; 14:40 KJV).

If Paul were to arrive on the scene today he would undoubtedly deal with us as he did with the Corinthians:

"My brothers and sisters, I hear there are divisions among you . . . for I hear some of you saying you are of Luther, and others, of Calvin, still others that you are of Peter, or of Wesley! Is Christ divided? Was Wesley crucified for you? Or were you baptized in the name of the Episcopal church?" Then Paul would turn to the charismatic groups—some of them, anyway—and say something like this:

"My dear brethren, I am so delighted to hear and see the wonderful gifts of the Spirit manifested among you. I couldn't understand where they had gone when I was with those other churches—but please! Did that brother have to shout quite so loudly? I saw someone walk out of the meeting when he did! You had a public meeting and invited unbelievers, and then all of you spoke in tongues at the same time with no explanation! Did that show love and concern for your visitors? I am sure some of the people you were trying to reach thought you were crazy! Remember that the spirit of the prophet is subject to the prophet, won't you?"

Can speaking in tongues be counterfeited? Of course. All the Gifts have their Satanic counterfeit, and there are certainly strange utterances and sounds made by those who worship other gods, or are involved in other religions or cults, that are a counterfeit of speaking in tongues. In a large public meeting, where it is difficult properly to control the situation, it might be possible for such a person to manifest a counterfeit. This is where the gift of discerning spirits is needed. No Christian, however, who is walking in the Spirit, under the protection of the Blood of Jesus, need fear that he or she might produce a counterfeit of speaking in tongues. The Scripture reminds us of our safety in Christ:

"If a son shall ask bread of any of you that is a father, will he give him a stone? or if he ask a fish, will he for a fish give him a serpent? If you then, being evil, know how to give good gifts unto your children; how much more shall your heavenly Father give the Holy Spirit to them that ask him?" (Luke 11:11, 13). ". . . . No man speaking by the Spirit of God (this can mean a Christian speaking in tongues) calls Jesus accursed" (I Cor. 12:3).

In summary, the gift of tongues and interpretation of tongues is first of all a sign to unbelievers (I Cor. 14:22), *when manifested according to scriptural instructions.* Secondly, these two gifts have the same benefit as prophecy and therefore are also for the edification of the Church (I Cor. 14:5, 26–27).

Ask God to use you in these two gifts; both are needed. The Apostle Paul, in I Corinthians 12, compares the publicly manifested gifts of the Spirit with the various members and senses of the body, each having its place, and each being necessary in its own way. In the light of this Scripture, it is hard to see how any of the gifts could be categorized as less or more significant than any other, since Paul emphasizes that each member of the body is important. Unless all the gifts are manifested, the Body of Christ on earth will be handicapped.

Each should examine his or her life, and make things right

with God before manifesting God's gifts. If people are helped, be sure to give God the glory! Pray that God's glory will be manifested through other members in the Body of Christ also (John 17:22).

8
The Gift of Prophecy

The gift of prophecy is manifested when believers speak the mind of God, by the inspiration of the Holy Spirit, and not from their own thoughts. It is supernatural speech in a known language. Prophecy is not a "private" gift, but is always brought to a group of believers although it may be for one or more individuals who are present. In this way it may be "judged," that is, evaluated by the Church.

Although prophecy is sixth on the list in I Corinthians 12, yet Paul puts it at the top in the fourteenth chapter, as being of the greatest benefit to the Church. He says:

"Follow after charity, and desire spiritual gifts, but rather that you may prophesy . . . he that prophesies edifies (builds up) the Church." The thirty-ninth verse is even more emphatic:

"*Covet* to prophesy!"

In the last chapter we saw that the gifts of tongues and interpretation together were first of all a sign to unbelievers, and secondly, to build up the Church—the believers. Prophecy is just the reverse, being first for the edification of the believers, and secondly for unbelievers. ". . . Prophecy serves not for them that believe not, but for those who believe" (I Cor. 14:22).

There are three ways, the Scripture tells us, in which prophecy ministers to believers: edification, exhortation, and comfort; or building up, urging on, and consoling (I Cor. 14:3). Obviously then, most prophecy to the Church is of an encouraging nature, but not all. If an earthly father never corrected his children, it would be harmful and unloving. They wouldn't grow up and mature normally. On the other hand, if the father were always telling them they were wrong, and never told them that he loved and appreciated them, love wouldn't grow between the parent and the children. We may say that there is a healthy ratio here: one-third exhortation and two-thirds comfort! Thus in a meeting you may expect to hear many prophecies that are frankly the Father comforting, and fewer that are of the "get with it" variety! Valid prophecy will not be harshly condemnatory of believers, but it may strongly counsel them.

Up to the present, in most charismatic meetings there has been more ministry to believers through the gifts of tongues and interpretation than through the gift of prophecy. One reason for this is that it seems to require more faith to speak out directly in prophecy, than for one person to speak in tongues and another to interpret. Speaking in tongues is an easier gift to bring than prophecy precisely because the language is unknown to the speaker and so he or she does not fear saying the wrong thing, and the interpretation is usually brought by another person. The person prophesying, however, has to carry the whole responsibility!

The first purpose of prophecy, thus, is to speak to believers, but this gift can also bring unbelievers to God. The Scripture says: "But if all prophesy, and there comes in one that does not believe, or one that is uninstructed, he is convinced of all, he is judged of all: and thus are the secrets of his heart made manifest; and so falling down on his face he will worship God, and report that God is in you of a truth" (I Cor. 14:24–25). This indicates the use of the gift of prophecy together with the gift of knowledge. This latter is briefly the divine revelation of facts not learned through the natural mind. We will talk about this gift in more detail in a later chapter. As these intimate facts are revealed about the condition of the unbeliever's heart, he is convinced of God's reality and immediately converted. The "unlearned" or uninstructed believer, on the other hand, who does not fully understand the gifts of the Spirit, not having received the baptism in the Holy Spirit, is often at this point convinced that these things are real. (This last is happening quite frequently today, of course. Many "uninstructed" believers are coming to receive the baptism in the Holy Spirit because they have seen the gifts in operation which they had been told were "not for today.")

In the Old Testament there were men who were moved of God to prophesy. These prophets were especially chosen of God to speak His word to the people, usually ministering the combined gifts of prophecy and knowledge, and often doing other "mighty acts" by the power of God. Many times God's will and intention were given through them. Usually any prophecy concerning the future had an "if" connected with it:

"In forty days Nineveh shall be overthrown" (Jonah 3:4), Jonah was commanded to announce. But the people of Nineveh repented in sackcloth and ashes. What would have been the point of bothering to send Jonah if there was no chance for them to repent? So Nineveh wasn't overthrown—at least, not at that time—and Jonah was very upset!

Jeremiah was a prophet of old who warned the cities of Judah to turn from the error of their ways. This was a "conditional" prophecy, too. After hearing him speak these words from the Lord, the priest, the other prophets, and the people wanted to kill Jeremiah. The role of the prophet was often unpopular, and sometimes very dangerous. "Which of the prophets have not your fathers persecuted?" Stephen challenged the Sanhedrin. Jesus cried: "O Jerusalem, Jerusalem, you who kill the prophets . . . !" (Matt. 23:37, Acts 7:52).

There are also many *un*conditional prophecies concerning God's definite plans, especially concerning the coming of Christ. Isaiah 53 is a perfect example—it is one of the greatest prophecies in the Old Testament concerning the Lord Jesus. Moses prophesied about Christ: "The Lord thy God will raise up unto thee a Prophet from the midst of thee, of thy brethren, like unto me; unto him ye shall hearken" (Deut. 18:15 KJV). And indeed Jesus Christ Himself was a "prophet mighty in deed and word" (Luke 24:19 KJV). He was *the* Prophet,[1] just as He was *the* Priest, and *the* King. We have many prophetic utterances by Jesus Christ in the New Testament. Mark 13 and Matthew 24, are strong prophecies of coming things. John 16 is almost entirely a prophecy through Jesus to His closest disciples:

"These things have I spoken unto you, that ye should not be offended. They shall put you out of the synagogues: yea, the time cometh, that whosoever killeth you will think that he doeth God service. And these things will they do unto you, because they have not known the Father, nor me. But these things I have told you, that when the time shall come, you may remember that I told you of them" (John 16:1-4). (Read the rest of the chapter, too.)

These "unconditional" prophecies are mainly given for guideposts to believers, so that we may discern the "signs of the times." Jesus said: "I tell you before it come to pass, that, when it is come to pass, you may believe" (John 14:29). We are not supposed to be arguing over the prophecies, but simply noting them as they come to pass, so that we know where we are in God's time plan.

In Old Testament times God could not yet, by His Spirit, come to *dwell in* His people, but the Holy Spirit did come down to anoint certain people as they were yielded to God. The Spirit rested on them. In one instance, Moses as a prophet and a leader of the Children of Israel found his work too heavy a load to carry alone, so God took of the Holy Spirit resting upon him and put the Spirit also upon seventy other men; when this happened, they too began to prophesy. Then a problem arose as two of the

---

[1] Just seeing Jesus as a Prophet does not make one a Christian; He must be recognized to be the divine Son of God, God made flesh!

brethren, Eldad and Medad, who were not with the rest of the seventy in the Tabernacle, also were inspired by the Spirit and began to prophesy in the open camp. Some of the others complained and wanted to forbid the two men to minister. Moses answer was in itself a prophecy:

"Are you envious for my sake? would God that all the Lord's people were prophets, and that the Lord would put his spirit upon them!" (Num. 11:29).

These words were fulfilled on the day of Pentecost. On that day Peter quoted the words of Joel which were similar: "This is that which was spoken by the prophet Joel; And it shall come to pass in the last days, says God, I will pour out of my Spirit upon all flesh: and your sons and your daughters shall prophesy, and your young men shall see visions, and your old men shall dream dreams: And on my servants and on my handmaidens I will pour out in those days of My Spirit; and they shall prophesy:" (Acts 2:16–18).

At Ephesus, when Paul laid hands on the twelve men and they received their "Pentecost," they "spoke with tongues and prophesied" (Acts 19:6). The Scripture tells us that ever since the day of Pentecost and the outpouring of the Holy Spirit, any yielded child of God may be moved by the Spirit to prophesy. Paul at Corinth, after urging them all to seek to prophesy, even refers to all those used this way as prophets: "Let the prophets speak two or three, and let the other (Greek—others) judge. If any thing be revealed to another that sitteth by, let the first hold his peace. For you may all prophesy one by one, that all may learn, and all may be comforted. And the spirits of the prophets are subject to the prophets" (I Cor. 14:29–32).

These verses also tell us the "rules" for the use of prophecy in a meeting. The prophets are to be limited to speaking two or three times—the same as for tongues and interpretation. As wonderful as the vocal gifts are, they must not take over the meeting. Plenty of room must be given to inspired teaching from the Word of God, to praise and prayer, to sharing of testimony, to singing God's praises, etc.

As we have said earlier, prophecy is always to the community: the people of God. It should always be brought in the presence of others, because prophecy is always to be judged or evaluated by the Church, in terms of the witness of the Spirit in the hearts of the other brethren, and in terms of the written Word of God, with which the prophecy must always agree. This provides the control, too, from an individual claiming too much for him or herself. The leader of the meeting must especially be sensitive to correct wherever it is needed. Good manners and consideration for others is also mentioned. "The spirits of the prophets are subject to the prophets" reminds us that the gifts of the Spirit are inspiration, not compulsion, and provide no excuse for erratic behavior. If the Holy Spirit is truly being followed, the meeting will be peaceful, loving, and orderly: "in decency and order," as Paul puts it. The word "decency" for us might better be translated "fittingly," or "becomingly."

Women are permitted to minister in prayer and prophecy as long as they are under "headship," that is, submitted to male leadership. We have found a sort of "semi-Pauline rule" to be effective, asking that two women do not minister one after another, but wait for a man to alternate, e.g., if a woman has spoken in tongues, to expect and wait for a man to bring the interpretation; if a woman brings a testimony or prophecy, to ask the other women to wait until a man has ministered before another woman does so. This kind of practice encourages both men and women, since there are very few ladies who don't want to see the men take the lead.

If a woman is in doubt as to her right to prophesy, let her remember the beautiful prophecy brought by Mary the mother of Jesus:

"My soul doth magnify the Lord, And my spirit hath rejoiced in God my Saviour. For he hath regarded the low estate of his handmaiden: for, behold, from henceforth all generations shall call me blessed. For he that is mighty hath done to me great things; and holy is his name. And his mercy is on them that fear him from generation to generation. He hath shewed strength with his arm; he hath scattered the proud in the imagination of their hearts. He hath put down the mighty from their seats, and exalted them of low degree. He hath filled the hungry with good things; and the rich he hath sent empty away" (Luke 1:46-53 KJV).

We have been talking about the gift of prophecy for all members of the Body, but now we need to talk about those who have a *ministry* in prophecy. Just as the Apostolic Age has not ended, and the ministry of the apostle is still going on today, so there are still those with the ministry of the prophet today. Because the Old Testament prophets often spoke out against social and political abuses, and against priestcraft and the hierarchy of that day—the "establishment!"—an erroneous idea has sprung up that every protester and militant campaigner for social justice is a "prophet," and that "prophecy" mainly consists in denouncing human evil. As we have seen, however, it isn't what a man says in the natural realm that makes him a prophet; it is the fact that he is moved by the Spirit of God to speak the words *God* gives him.

The real prophet will not find it necessary to announce to others that he is a prophet; he will be known by his ministry. Moses is a strong example of a prophet, yet the Bible says of him: "Moses was very meek (humble, gentle), above all the men which were upon the face of the earth" (Num. 12:3 KJV). This is a good test for the prophet today. A prophet of God will naturally minister in the gift of prophecy often, and it will very likely be conjoined to the gift of knowledge—it is often hard to distinguish between the two—declaring God's will and God's mind. When Jesus told the woman at the well about her personal life in detail, she immediately said:

"Sir, I perceive that you are a prophet" (John 4:19).

A true prophet of God will be a mature Christian, as his ministry is listed as one of the offices to be used to bring the Church to maturity (Eph. 4:8, 11–16). No person should be allowed to minister as an established prophet in the Church unless he is thoroughly known by the brethren as to his doctrine and his manner of life. A true prophet will speak out against things that are wrong, whether it makes him unpopular or not. He will draw people to God and not to himself.

The ministry of the prophet must be even more carefully judged than that of the brethren in general who prophesy in the meeting. A man may be strongly used in the prophetic office, and yet may be completely wrong from time to time. His words must never be accepted because of his ministry, but tested by the Word and the Spirit; this does not mean at all that he is a false prophet, but that he is still not perfected and therefore liable to error. "We prophesy in part" (I Cor. 13:9 KJV).

The enemy has counterfeits of all the true gifts, and there are plenty of false prophets in the world. A false prophet is a most dangerous person, as he will use his supposed authority to gain wrong influence over people, and keep them in bondage to himself through fear. He will separate them from others in the family of Christ lest he be challenged and found out, using as an excuse that they are a very special and elite group. Recently in our own city a small group of earnest Christians was taken over by a man from another city. He came in and told them that he was to be their "shepherd." They were to have no contact even with relatives and friends who did not approve of the group, and were to read no other literature than that which he permitted them to read—most of which he had written himself! They were, of course, to listen to no other teachers but himself. If anyone separated himself from the group, he would be lost, they were told. There are many such "grievous wolves," as Paul called them, preying upon God's people today, so be warned.

"Thus saith the LORD of hosts, Hearken not unto the words of the prophets that prophesy unto you: *they make you vain:* they speak a vision of their own heart, and not out of the mouth of the LORD" (Jer. 23:16 KJV). The deceiving prophet will not warn the people to turn from that which is wrong (Jer. 23:17–22), and usually immorality springs up where there is false prophecy.

We should also be careful of personal, directive prophecy, especially outside the ministry of a mature and submitted man of God. Unrestrained "personal prophecy" did much to undermine the movement of the Holy Spirit which began at the turn of the century. It is still present today. Christians are certainly given words for one another "in the Lord," of knowledge or wisdom, and such words can be most refreshing and helpful, but there must be a witness of the Spirit on the part of the person receiving the words, and extreme caution should be used in receiving any alleged directive or predictive prophecy. Never undertake any project simply because you were told to by presumed prophetic utterance or interpretation of tongues, or by a presumed word of wisdom, or knowledge. Never do something just because a friend comes to you and says: "The Lord told me to tell you to do thus and thus!" If the Lord has instructions for you, He will give you a witness in your own heart, in which case the words coming from a friend, or through the gifts of the Holy Spirit in a meeting, will be confirmation to what God *has already been* showing you. Your guidance must also agree with Scripture. Speaking of the Scriptures, Peter says:

"We have a more sure Word of Prophecy; whereunto you do well that you take heed, as unto a light that shines in a dark place, until the day dawn, and the day star arise in your hearts . . ." (II Pet. 1:19). The written Word of God is our guidebook, which we must study well, and is the test of all spoken words. There is an old saying which bears repeating: "If you have the Spirit without the Word, you'll blow up; if you have the Word without the Spirit, you'll dry up; but if you have the Spirit and the Word, you'll grow up!"

Note the caution of the prophet Jeremiah. He was told by the Lord to buy a piece of property from his cousin Hanameel. He took no action, however, until his cousin came and offered to sell him the property, having no idea what the Lord had already said to Jeremiah. "Then," said Jeremiah, "I knew it was the word of the Lord." If the prophet Jeremiah, that great man of God, was so cautious, not even believing his own prophecy until it was confirmed, we should be all the more (Jer. 32:6-9).

Prophecy isn't fortune-telling! Prophecy isn't looking into a crystal ball, or reading cards or supposedly predicting the future by any other method. As we have already said in detail in a previous chapter, God strictly forbids any attempt to pry into the future—He has always forbidden it. If men attempt to do this, they will be fed information from the enemy for his own purposes, and if they persist, it will be to their destruction. As we have seen, it is true that the Scripture shows that through the utterances of His prophets God sometimes tells what is going to happen; however, this has nothing whatsoever to do with fortune-telling; God has simply shared His intentions with His faithful children. The true prophet was not *trying to get* information about the present or the future, but he was having fellowship with the Lord, when God chose to share the knowledge. True prophecy is *forth*telling not *fore*telling.

Prophecy is not *"inspired preaching."* Preaching, which means "proclaiming the Gospel," should indeed be inspired by the Holy Spirit, but in preaching, the intellect, training, skill, background, and education are involved and inspired by the Holy Spirit. The sermon may be written down ahead of time, or given on the spot, but it comes from the inspired intellect. Prophecy, on the other hand, means that the person is bringing the words the Lord gives directly; it is from the spirit, not the intellect. A person can bring prophetic words that he does not even understand himself. In the course of an inspired sermon, the preacher may also prophesy, or manifest the gifts of wisdom and knowledge, but they are to be distinguished from *preaching*.

Prophecy is not *witnessing*. Some, trying to justify the lack of prophecy in the Church today, say that it is. They quote the Scripture: "The testimony of Jesus is the spirit of prophecy." Although it is true that the Holy Spirit wants us to witness to unbelievers and has given us the power to do so, yet how could this be "prophecy," when prophecy is the greatest gift to edify the *Church?*

Paul, in his first letter to the Thessalonians, says: "Don't despise prophesying. Prove all things; hold fast that which is good" (I Thess. 5:20-21). Just because there is misuse of God's gifts, and the enemy has counterfeits, doesn't mean we should reject what God has for us. That's exactly what the enemy would want. When the children of Israel came out of the wilderness into the promised land, they found the fruit to be much bigger, but the enemy was, too! There were giants in the land, along with grapes of Eschol, and we may find this true as we enter this new walk in the Spirit—but the fruit is worth the effort required!

Jesus is Prophet, Priest, and King. We today, through Him, can also have these ministries as prophets, priests, and kings (Rev. 1:6). A prophet speaks the words of God to the people; a priest speaks to God on behalf of the people, in praise and prayer; and a king rules, taking authority by his words over the works of the enemy. In all three ministries the *voice* is extremely important, and gives us further insight into why the *voice* must be yielded at Pentecost. If we desire to bring the gifts of utterance, let us keep our lips from speaking evil, for God says of those who do: "You shall be as my mouth" (Jer. 15:19 RSV).

Expect to prophesy. Ask Jesus to edify His Body on earth through you. As you have fellowship with the Lord and with your brothers and sisters in the Lord, you may find thoughts and words of inspiration coming into your mind that you have not heard, and did not compose. If they are according to Scripture, then share them with the Church. As with interpretation, you may just receive a few words, and as you start to speak, more may come. You may see a picture in your "mind's eye," and as you start to talk about that picture, the words will come. As with tongues and interpretation, the Spirit may bring you the words in a variety of ways. Some also have seen the words as if written down, and just read them *verbatim*.

The gifts are manifested through God's ability, not ours. He will give the faith that is needed, if He has given you some words to speak (Rom. 12:6). Don't be afraid to bring a prophecy, nor feel sensitive about the fact that the Church must evaluate it. Don't quench the Spirit. The prophet Amos asks: "The Lord God hath spoken, who can but prophesy?" (Amos 3:8 KJV). Forget your pride, and testify to Jesus!

9
Gifts of Healing

The gifts of power are healing, miracles, and faith. They are the continuation of Jesus' compassionate ministry to those in need. Most everyone is interested in the gifts of healing since the need is so widespread. This is one of the most obviously beneficial gifts to man in this life. It is the most widely accepted of the nine gifts of the Holy Spirit in Christendom today. The Lord Jesus brought this gift into prominence in that ninety percent of His recorded ministry on earth was spent healing the sick. His first instruction to His disciples was:

"Heal the sick!" (Matt. 10:8).

Yet after His Resurrection and before His Ascension there is no record of His healing anyone. During this forty days He spent much time teaching and preparing His disciples further to carry on the ministry He had begun. So immediately after Pentecost we find the first believers continuing the ministry of Jesus in healing the sick, raising the dead, and casting out evil spirits. Jesus' healing ministry has been going on now for nearly two thousand years, and will continue until He Himself returns to this earth. Jesus gave us this great promise: "He that believes in me, the works that I do he shall do also; and greater works than these shall he do; because I go unto my Father!" (John 14:12).

The gifts of healing are for the supernatural curing of injuries, handicaps, and diseases without the aid of natural means or human skills. They are manifestations of the Holy Spirit working through compassionate human channels to the person in need. Those who are used as channels of God's healing should not claim to "have" these gifts, nor should they claim to be "healers," but rather should realize that any of the nine gifts could be manifested through them as the Holy Spirit moves to meet the needs around them. There is a real interdependence between God and man in the gifts of the Spirit. For instance, if you felt God wanted you to pray for a friend, you would get in the car, drive to your friend's house, go in and tell how Jesus heals today, pray with your friend, and Jesus would do the healing. Some onlooker could say: "It looks as though you were doing the whole thing." Actually you were a "witness" first, telling what Jesus would do; then you were a "delivery boy," bringing the gift from Jesus, through the Holy Spirit in you. God guides us and uses our work, but He is the Healer. We are privileged to be co-workers together with the Lord Jesus. After the Ascension and Pentecost, the Scripture says that the disciples: "Went forth, and preached every where, *the Lord working with them, and confirming the word with signs following*" (Mark 16:20 KJV).

A Christian does not have to have the baptism with the Holy Spirit in order to pray for the sick, nor is the fact that a person has prayed effectively for the sick a sign that he or she has received the baptism with the Holy Spirit. Jesus said: "These signs shall follow them that *believe* . . . they shall lay hands on the sick, and they shall recover" (Mark 16:17–18 KJV). Any *believer* can pray for the sick and see them healed by the power of Jesus. Generally speaking, however, it is after the baptism in the Holy Spirit that increased faith for healing comes, and the Christian begins to minister to the sick. Like the other gifts, healing seems to be released with a far greater intensity and reality after the receiving of the Holy Spirit.

The "laying on of hands" usually means touching the sick person's head with one or both hands as you pray. Laying on of hands is not magic, but it is scriptural. It provides a "point of contact" for the sick person to "release his faith" as Oral Roberts puts it. It also can be a channel for real Spiritual power. The Bible says that we may lay hands on the sick, and so we do. However, notice also the great variety of ways in which the Lord Jesus prayed for the sick. Sometimes He laid hands on them, at times on their eyes or ears; sometimes He made no outward gesture, but just spoke the word and they were healed. Often He commanded *them* to do something as an act of faith. Once He put mud on a blind man's eyes, and told him to go wash it off! Another time He simply said to some lepers: "Go and show yourselves to the priests" (the health department), and as they turned to go they were healed! This, by the way, should be noted by those who are suffering from diseases that need to be controlled with medication. We do not encourage people to discontinue such medication (for epilepsy, diabetes, heart trouble, etc., for example) until they have "gone and showed themselves to the priests"—the doctors—and their cure has been verified. The same would apply to a person suffering from tuberculosis, or other communicable diseases, who is healed by Jesus through the gift of healing.

In the Epistle of James we read of healing in conjunction with "anointing with oil" (Jas. 5:14–15) in answer to believing prayer. The elders, the leaders of the congregation, are to anoint with oil as they pray for the sick of that particular congregation. The disciples anointed with oil as they prayed for the sick (Mark 6:13). Oil is one of the symbols of the Holy Spirit in the Bible. "Anointing" meant to pour oil (usually olive oil) on the sick person as prayer was said. Today the usual custom is to touch the forehead of the sick person with the oil. The Epistle of James goes on to say: "The prayer of faith *shall* save (heal) the sick, and the Lord *shall* raise him up . . ." (Jas. 5:15 KJV). Note the unconditional nature of the promise! We have no scriptural warrant to end a healing prayer with the faith-destroying phrase, "If it be Thy will"! God has made it perfectly clear in His Word that it *is* His will to heal the sick—period! Jesus never prayed for the sick in a conditional manner. He tells us that we must believe that we have received the answer to our prayer even before we pray! (Mark 11:24). Some remind us that Jesus prayed in Gethsemane "If it by Thy will"—or rather, "Not My will but Thine." This is an entirely different situation. Jesus knew the Father's will. He had come to earth for just that purpose, that He should die for our sins, and be raised for our justification. He was praying about His own unwillingness to be separated from loving fellowship with His Father as would occur during those painful hours on the Cross when He took the sins of the world upon Himself.

In the case of healing, we know the Father's will: "I am the Lord Jehovah thy God that healeth thee!" (Exod. 15:26). "Who healeth all thy diseases" (Ps. 103:3 KJV). "I will take sickness away from the midst of thee!" (Exod. 23:25 KJV).

Some people feel that Jesus would heal, but they are not sure about the Father! Dennis was asked to call on a woman who was very seriously ill—the doctors said she was dying and there was nothing to be done.

Entering the room, he could see that she was very ill indeed. She was pale and emaciated, yet she had a beautiful glow in her face. She said to him, with a smile: "It's all right. I'm reconciled to the fact that this is God's will!"

What could he say? Here he had been sent to pray for her recovery, and she was sure that God wanted her to die! He said to her:

"I can't argue with you at a time like this, but please answer me one question—if Jesus Himself were to walk into this room what would He do?"

With scarely a moment's hesitation, she replied:

"Why, He'd *heal* me!"

Dennis nodded. "You don't have any doubt of that, do you?" She shook her head. "No."

"Well," he said, "Jesus said that He only did the things He saw His Father do—that He did nothing of Himself (John 5:19). He also said that He and His Father were so close, as to be like One—that if we had seen Him, we had seen His Father. How can you tell me that Jesus would heal you, but the Father wills that you die of this disease?"

She thought a moment, then her face brightened even more.

"I see what you mean!" she said. Then they could pray for healing.

A woman shared this story with us: "When I was seriously ill quite a few people prayed with me, but they always added the words: 'If it be Thy will, Lord.' And each time, my heart would sink when I heard this phrase. The day I was healed was when someone prayed with real faith. I kept waiting to see *if* they too would say 'If it be Thy will,' but praise God, they didn't!" If we can't pray with assurance and faith for the sick, we should wait until we can, or pray that God will send someone else who can.

We do not need to make long prayers for the sick. When we have the faith to say it, a word of command can be effective: "Be healed, in Jesus' Name!" Jesus healed with a touch, or a word—most often with a command: "Be thou clean!" He said to the leper. To the "sick of the palsy" He said: "Get up, pick up your mat, and go to your house!" To the deaf man's ears He commanded: "Be opened!" To the man with the withered hand He said: "Stretch forth your hand!" and it was instantly healed.

Note that in the list in I Corinthians 12:9 Paul speaks of "gifts" of healing, not just "the gift" of healing. Three times in this chapter it is mentioned, and each time the two nouns are plural in the Greek. The words are actually translated "gifts of cures." This is logical. Since there are many diseases, many gifts of healing are needed. One of the most wonderful of the healing promises concerning Jesus our Healer is this: "He was wounded for our transgressions, he was bruised for our iniquities: the chastisement of our peace was upon him; and with his stripes we are healed" (Isa. 53:5 KJV). Or, as Peter says, looking back at the crucifixion, and we say it with him: "By whose stripes ye *were* healed" (I Pet. 2:24 KJV). Thirty-nine stripes were laid on Jesus' back, and they represent healing for *all* our diseases.

As with the other gifts, some Christians are given a *ministry* of healing—being used often in this way. It is not unusual for this ministry to be stronger in praying successfully for one type of ailment than another. For example, one friend of ours has a strong ministry to arthritics, another for dental problems, etc. Perhaps this is what Paul means by "gifts of healing." Some have developed large and well-known ministries in this area, and thousands have been, and are being, healed and helped. We are deeply thankful for these dedicated and yielded people. It will be even more wonderful, though, when large numbers of God's children begin to move out for Him, and obey the command to "heal the sick." In every local congregation where the baptism in the Holy Spirit is being received, there are people with undeveloped ministries of healing.

A person can be healed through another's faith when he is too ill and weak to exercise his own faith (Mark 2:3–5), though he may be unconscious or in a coma. Healing can come through the faith (in Jesus) of the sick person alone (Matt. 9:22, 29), or with the combined faith of the sick person and the one ministering (Mark 5:25–34). This last of course is the most desirable situation. It is important to take time to build the faith of the sick person, when at all possible, before laying on hands for healing. This may be done by sharing with him or her the Scripture about healing, and by sharing personal testimonies. As the Apostle Paul tells the Romans, "Faith comes by hearing, and hearing by the Word of God" (Rom. 10:17). Impress the fact that we need not even depend on the faith of others, but stand squarely on God's Word.

Rita was sharing her testimony with a group of women in a private home in Spokane, Washington, in 1965, when her hostess' telephone rang. It was a lady by the name of Juanita Beeman. Rita was introduced to her over the phone, and was informed of her need. Juanita had a rapid heart which had required the installation of an electronic "pacemaker" so that it would beat normally. Although it was some months after the surgery to implant this device, she was still flat in bed. Her heart was enlarged, and every two weeks the fluid which collected around the heart had to be removed. She asked if Rita would come and pray for her. The next morning Rita went to hear a visiting evangelist preach on faith. He shared the Scriptures one after the other with real conviction and her own faith was greatly built up. Following this she went to the Beemans' home, and when she met the couple she could tell they were real believers. After sharing the Scripture on healing and talking about different healings she had seen, they prayed. God's presence was so strong that all of them were moved to tears. Several days later, when Juanita *walked* into the doctor's office (she had previously had to be taken in a wheelchair because of her weakness), the doctor asked in surprise: "What's happened to you?" She replied happily: "God answers prayer, doctor!" He tested and examined her, and found that her heart had returned to normal size, and that there was no fluid to be removed. Juanita has been leading a joyful and active life ever since.

When you pray for the sick, both you and the sick person should be edified. Smith Wigglesworth said that he never felt God's power more strongly than when he was praying for the sick. He often had a vision of Jesus in the course of an earnest healing prayer. He found that the atmosphere and surroundings in which the prayer is said are important.

We are sure we have watched a patient literally "murdered" by television, when he had his eyes glued to it and could scarcely be persuaded to turn the device off in order to receive prayer for healing! If you have control over the situation, insist that all possible distraction be removed, not only during the time of prayer, but especially *afterward*, and if possible, before. Wigglesworth, again, would ask all unbelievers to leave, if he possibly could, before praying for healing. Note that Jesus did this at the raising of Jairus' daughter (Mark 5:38–40). Of course all these things should be done with charity. (We recommend strongly that you read the life of Smith Wigglesworth in the books *Ever Increasing Faith*, and *Smith Wigglesworth, Apostle of Faith*. They are good faith-builders for healing. There are many others.)

The one who feels led to pray for the sick should take time to ask God how He would have him proceed. Other gifts of the Spirit such as the word of knowledge and the word of wisdom should be expected to be manifested in conjunction with the gifts of healing. There may be something in the sick person's life that is stopping the healing, and that could be revealed by the word of knowledge.

The gift of the word of knowledge can be a great faith-builder. At times the Lord will show to one Christian that another has a certain physical need. As this is shared, it will give the sick person tremendous assurance and faith to reach out and receive his healing. Several healing evangelists depend heavily on the word of knowledge to build faith, and as the Lord reveals the needs, people are healed right where they are sitting or standing with no need of any to minister to them individually but the Lord Himself.

Faith is of course the most important of the gifts for the healing ministry. There are times when the gift of faith will be so strong that you will *know*, before you pray, that the person is to be healed.

It is important to explain to the sick person that as hands are laid on him, he should release his faith and receive his healing. As we have said, God's healing can come by a touch, a word, or any other action of faith. Some people have been healed by touching the radio when an evangelist is speaking about healing. This happened recently in the course of our own radio broadcast in Seattle, even though we had never suggested it. A listener touched her radio, released her faith, and was healed! People who are far away have been healed through the prayers of friends (Matt. 8:8), even though they did not know the friends were praying! One day a group of Episcopalians in Van Nuys, California, was praying for a friend who had a terribly abscessed tooth. As they prayed, the telephone rang.

"What's going on over there?" the woman asked. "My jaw was just instantly healed!" The Scripture records other unusual cases of healing by the passing of a person's shadow over the sick (Acts 5:15)—or by handkerchiefs or aprons being brought that had been touched by the person God was using in a ministry of healing (Acts 19:11–12). Needless to say, any of these things can be abused or misused, but they certainly are real and valid. Again, they are occasions for the release of faith. We know of cases today where someone has brought a blessed handkerchief and placed it in contact with a sick person—unbeknownst to him —and he has been healed! Here it is the faith of the person bringing the blessed object that provides the channel for God's healing.

We know from the Scripture that God wants His people to be whole in spirit, soul, and body. As wonderful as physical healing, is, we still know that our life on this planet, as we know it, is but a drop in the ocean of eternity. The most important healing is, of course, the healing of soul and spirit, for this has eternal value. Many times, however, when the inner man is touched by God in salvation, there is a chain reaction in which God's wholeness touches the soul and body with health. The Book of Romans says: "If you confess with your mouth the Lord Jesus and believe in your heart that God has raised Him from the dead, you shall be saved" (Rom. 10:9). The Greek word here translated "saved" is *sozo*, which means to be healed, saved from danger, kept in safety, or saved from eternal death. It is an all-encompassing word, that applies not only to the spirit, but to the soul and body also. When Ananias prayed for Paul, he was healed and baptized in the Holy Spirit almost simultaneously (Acts 9:17–18). This has been known to happen today. Praying in the language the Holy Spirit gives (speaking in tongues) can also bring healing, as the Spirit guides us to pray for our infirmities and ailments, or for the needs of others (Rom. 8:26).

We have quoted from James 5 the directions to anoint the sick with oil and to pray the prayer of faith. We also note that James says: "If he has committed sins, they shall be forgiven him" (Jas. 5:15). Sickness, like death, came as a result of the fall of man. But the Lord Jesus made it very clear that not all sickness is the direct result of sin in the individual's life. The disciples asked him about the blind man, in John 9: "Who did sin, this man or his parents, that he was born blind?" Jesus' answer is definite: "Neither has this man sinned, nor his parents: but that the works of God should be shown in him" (John 9:3).

On other occasions, however, Jesus makes a direct connection between the individual's sin and his sickness, and begins His healing by forgiving the sin. In Luke 18 we read how a paralyzed man was brought by four friends to Jesus. Jesus' first action is to say: "Man, your sins are forgiven you!" He then commands him to get up and walk.

In John 5, Jesus heals another paralytic, and this time warns him: "Sin no more, lest a worse thing come upon you!" (John 5:14).

In praying for the sick we must be aware that unrepented sin, a deep-held resentment, or a seriously wrong attitude, can prevent healing. The *Book of Common Prayer*, in the service for the visitation of the sick, directs:

"Then shall the sick person be moved to make a special confession of his sins, if he feel his conscience troubled with any matter, after which confession, on evidence of his repentance, the Minister shall assure him of God's mercy and forgiveness." [1] It is always a good policy, before praying with a sick person, to inquire of him whether his "conscience is troubled with any matter," and if so, to help him to come to repentance, and to confess his sin, in the manner to which he is accustomed.[2]

Wherever the Holy Spirit moves, there will be healing. God is not glorified in the sickness of His people, as is sometimes erroneously taught, but in their healing. When Paul tells us that he "glories in his infirmities" (which does not necessarily mean physical weakness or sickness) he means that his weakness is an occasion to show God's strength. Men are led to Jesus through seeing His healing today just as they were in New Testament days. Physical healing of the unbeliever should bring him to Jesus as

---

[1] *Book of Common Prayer*, p. 313.

[2] There is, of course, a great difference of opinion among various Christian groups as to how confession should be handled. Some feel that it is to be made to God alone, others believe that confession must be made in the presence of a priest. It is our belief that confession to an elder (presbyter, priest) was substituted for confession to the whole church, and that it concerned sins that affected the whole community—that is, open scandal—in which the elder could speak God's forgiveness on behalf of the whole church in a matter that would not be fitting to confess openly. We believe that the command "confess your faults one to another" is sound practice, and that the authority to declare God's forgiveness belongs to the ministry of every believer. Therefore if the person you are praying with has no pastoral relationship with any church, and no custom concerning confession, we suggest that you either direct him to your own minister or priest, or that you assist him in offering his sins to God, and then give him assurance of God's forgiveness in some such words as these: "I have heard you confess your sins to God, and I know you are truly repentant. I assure you by the Word of God, that God has forgiven you your sins, for He says: 'If we confess our sins, he is faithful and just to forgive us our sins, and to cleanse us from all unrighteousness'" (I John 1:9 KJV).

Anything said in your hearing during this time of confession is to be kept in *absolute* confidence, under the "seal of the confessional," which forbids even your speaking to the person himself about anything he has confessed, unless you have his permission. Simply forget what you have heard. God has taken care of it.

his Savior. Because through the years, and still today, so many Christian churches have failed to proclaim the truth that Jesus still heals today, false cults have sprung up around an unbiblical kind of healing that does not glorify Jesus. Someone has called these groups the "unpaid bills of the Church"! We have discussed them at length in chapter four.

On the other hand, many churches of all denominations who are moving in the charismatic dimension are seeing more and more healing. Blind eyes are opened; cataracts dissolved (yes, and even empty eye sockets filled!); deaf ears are made to hear; tumors disappear; broken bones are instantly mended; damaged hearts restored; multiple sclerosis, tuberculosis, cancer, paralysis, arthritis, and all the ills the flesh is heir to can be and are being healed by the touch of the Master's Hand. Some of these healings have been instantaneous, some progressive, some partial. In situations where we have desired to see healing, and we have not seen it, the fault is not with God, but with man. We are quick to say: "God didn't do it. I guess He isn't ready to heal me." Yet the Word of God says that He is, and right now.[3]

People say: "I'd believe in healing if I saw a case where the doctor took an x-ray, prayer was said, then a second x-ray was taken and healing proved!" There are many such cases on record, where the healing is completely proven by medical evidence, with all the x-rays, tests, etc., on file.[4] Alas, those who say they demand such evidence never seem to go and look at it! Jesus said: "If they believe not Moses and the Prophets (who certainly bore witness

[3] The Scriptures promise health for the believer. On the other hand, for a variety of reasons, believers sometimes get sick. The promise, however, is that if we become ill, God will heal us. People say: "You're not going to live forever. You've got to die sometime!" True. But long life is promised to God's people, and when we do go home to our Father, it is not necessary that we go in disease and pain. We read in Genesis 25:8, that: "Then Abraham gave up the ghost, and died in a good old age, an old man, and full of years; and was gathered to his people."

[4] Bennett, *op. cit.*, p. 199.

to God's healing), neither will they believe, though one rose from the dead" (Luke 16:31).

The best way to learn about healing is to begin to pray for the sick. Ask God to use you in this way, then step out in faith. Some know when they are to pray for the sick by an inner witness; others may feel a warmth in their hands; still others may have an overwhelming compassion. We should not depend only on these outward signs, however, but if they confirm that inner knowing in your spirit, you have double witness to claim God's healing, especially if circumstances make it possible for you to pray for the needy one. When healing takes place, be sure to give God the glory, and lead the healed one to Jesus if he or she hasn't already met Him. As you continue to look to our Lord Jesus and stay in loving fellowship with Him, the signs will follow.

10
The Working of Miracles

Miracles are events that seem to override or contradict the so-called laws of nature. There aren't any "laws of nature," actually. The concept of physical "laws" has been discarded by the modern physicist, who defines natural events in terms of "probability." For example, the old Newtonian physics said:

"There is a *law* that, neglecting air resistance, all objects fall with an acceleration of thirty-two feet per second, per second." Modern science would state it: "it is *probable* that all falling objects will accelerate at the rate of thirty-two feet per second, per second. This seems to be the way it happens!" And this comes very close to what the Christian says: "The so-called laws of nature codified by human science are simply God's usual way of doing things." He keeps things regular for our convenience. How awkward it would be to live in a universe where nothing happened twice the same way! It would be an Alice-in-Wonderland world, indeed, and very confusing! God, however, for His believing people, will change His accustomed ways of doing things, to meet their needs, and thus, too, show them that He is sovereign, and has all power. The great miracles of the Old and New Testaments were done to meet the needs of people, and to show them that God is real, and in full control of the situation!

It is not always easy to draw a sharp line between the gift of miracles and the gifts of healing. It would seem that "healing" should include those acts of power that involve the curing of a condition in the living human body (or animal body, for healing also can take place in animals by prayer). Other events would come under the heading of miracles.

Some of the typical miracles of the Old Testament are: the dividing of the Red Sea for the escape of the children of Israel (Exod. 14:21–31); the sun and moon standing still for Joshua (Josh. 10:12–14); the widow's cruse of oil and barrel of meal that did not run out through the time of famine (I Kings 17:8–16); the descent of the fire on Mt. Carmel to consume Elijah's sacrifice and reveal the true God (I Kings 18:17–39); the sun going backward ten degrees on Hezekiah's sundial in response to Isaiah's prayer (II Kings 20:8–11); the miraculous plagues of Egypt (Exod. 7–12); the pot of poisonous soup which was made harmless through Elisha's act of faith (II Kings 4:38–41). The greatest number of miracles in the Old Testament are recorded in the lives of Moses, Elijah, and Elisha.

The record of Elijah and his disciple, Elisha, speaks to us today. Elisha asked that he might have a "double portion" of the Holy Spirit that rested upon Elijah. As Elijah was caught up into heaven, his mantle—symbolic of his anointing—fell upon Elisha (II Kings 2:9–14). Sure enough, the Scripture records that Elisha did twice as many miracles as Elijah! This is symbolic of what happened to believers after Jesus' ascension, although Jesus did not bequeath just a "double portion" of His Spirit—He set no limit. He simply said: "Greater works than these shall ye do, because I go to My Father!" (John 14:12).

The gift of miracles is one of the gifts which brings much glory to God, and one which should be seen today more than ever before—according to Jesus' promise. God delights in doing miracles, and in using His children in this gift. The power to do *greater* works comes from the fact that Jesus ascended into heaven, and the full power of the Holy Spirit was sent at Pentecost, and has been available to Christians ever since.

Jesus, of course, performed more miracles than anyone else in the Bible, and apparently not all of them are recorded. As John said: "And there are also many other things . . . Jesus did . . . which, if they should be written every one, I suppose that even the world itself could not contain the books that should be written" (John 21:25 KJV). Some examples of His miracles found in the Scriptures include: turning water into wine (John 2:1–11), walking on water (Matt. 14:25–33), the miraculous feeding of the multitude (Mark 6:38–44; Matt. 16:8–10), causing the storm to cease (Mark 6:45–52), directing the disciples to catch fish where there had been none (John 21:5–12), and sending Peter to find money in the fish's mouth (Matt. 17:27).

Jesus' first miracle was turning water into wine: "This beginning of miracles did Jesus in Cana of Galilee, and manifested forth his glory; and his disciples believed on him" (John 2:11 KJV). Jesus' miracles were performed primarily out of His compassion to meet human needs, and for practical purposes. When He walked on water, He wanted to comfort His disciples; He needed to get there in a hurry. When He miraculously fed the multitudes, it was because food was not available otherwise. When He turned water into wine, it was because there was a need at the wedding reception. It is well to note, too, that the miracles were not done to force or frighten unbelievers into believing—they were done to encourage those who already believed or wanted to believe. Jesus said: "A wicked and adulterous generation seeketh after a sign, and no sign shall be given it, but the sign of the prophet Jonah (referring to His death and resurrection)" (Matt. 12:39–40). People say: "There you are! You're not supposed to have signs!" overlooking the fact that Jesus is talking to the "wicked and adulterous generation." On the other hand Jesus said:

"These signs *shall* follow them that *believe* . . ." (Mark 16:17 KJV).

Following Pentecost many signs of power were done by or for the apostles and others: several times believers were set free from prison by angelic power (Acts 12:1–17; 16:25–40; 5:17–25); the Evangelist Philip was transported bodily from Gaza to Azotus by the power of the Holy Spirit (Acts 8:39–40). (Please note! This was not "astral projection," or "astral" anything else. Philip was *physically* and *bodily* picked up by the Holy Spirit and carried from Gaza to Azotus, a distance of twenty-four miles!) Paul miraculously struck Elymas the Sorcerer with a temporary blindness in order to keep him from opposing the Gospel (Acts 13:8–12). Paul was bitten by a deadly snake, but took no harm from it (Acts 28:3–6).

Peter and Paul have the greatest number of miracles recorded in the Acts of the Apostles, but Stephen and Philip also performed miracles, and of course in I Corinthians 12 the gift of miracles is spoken of as one of the nine gifts that were regularly manifested by believers.

What did Jesus mean when He said that those who believe in Him would do "greater things"? Some think it means that there will be many *more* miracles due to the greater number of people who are filled with the Holy Spirit today. Others think it could also mean new miracles will be done in addition to, and even greater than, those recorded in the Bible. One thing is sure, that if Jesus meant that believers would do new miracles, they would be according to the pattern already set by the Lord, and would be according to the Scripture. There are plenty of weird events taking place these days, as men and women experiment with the occult and the psychic, that is to say with the powers of Satan, and the Christian must not be deceived by them. The Scripture tells us that the followers of the enemy will do "great signs and wonders; insomuch that, if it were possible, they shall deceive the very elect" (Matt. 24:24 KJV; Mark 13:22).

However, miracles are happening today according to the pattern of the Scriptures. In the book, *Nine O'Clock in the Morning,* we cited several cases in which God strikingly altered the weather in response to believing prayer.[1] There are present-day examples of persons being transported physically in the Spirit as Philip the Evangelist was in Acts 8:39–40. David duPlessis, perhaps the best-known witness in the charismatic renewal, tells of such a miracle in his earlier ministry. He and some other men were gathered in the garden outside a friend's home, praying for another man who was lying in bed, seriously ill, about a mile away.

"As we prayed," says David, "the Lord said to me: 'You are needed at that man's bedside *right away!*' I snatched up my hat and rushed 'round the house and out the front gate, but as I took one step out of the gate, my next step fell on the front steps of the house a mile away, where our sick friend was! It startled me greatly of course. I know that I was carried that mile instantly, because some fifteen minutes later the rest of the men I had been praying with came puffing down the road. They asked me: 'How did you get here so fast?' "

David needed to get there immediately so God simply provided his transportation!

In the last few years, what is perhaps the most powerful revival of New Testament Christianity the world has ever seen is taking place in Indonesia. Well-documented reports have been coming from there of miraculous events of the same nature and magnitude as in the Bible.[2] Thousands have been miraculously fed on provisions for a few hundred, water has been turned to wine for the purpose of Holy Communion, groups of Christians have walked on water in order to cross rivers to proclaim the good news of Christ, to say nothing of thousands healed, and many even raised from the dead.[3] One might dismiss these reports as fanciful, ex-

[1] Bennett, *op. cit.*, pp. 101–3.
[2] "South Pacific. Scene of Miracles Today," *Christian Life Magazine*, April, 1968.
[3] "Indonesia: The Greatest Work of God in the World Today," *Acts Magazine* I, no. 3. 1967. (We are saving the topic of the raising of the dead for the following chapter.)

cept they are confirmed by reliable witnesses, and often by Christians who did not previously believe that such New Testament miracles could or would take place today. Perhaps the strongest indirect evidence of the truth of these signs, is that over two and one-half million Moslems have accepted Christ, as well as thousands of Communists. The Moslem press recently admitted to the conversion of two million Mohammedans to the Christian faith! One of the big reasons undoubtedly is that they are seeing the power of God manifested, not only in the miracle of changed lives, but in the literal miracles of the Bible. Why should such amazing events be taking place? It is because people in Indonesia have never been told that certain parts of the Bible are "not for today"; therefore they are putting it into practice in simple faith! It works! God is alive!

God takes real chances when He shares His supernatural works with His people. He would no doubt work more miracles among His people but knows that unless we are spiritually prepared it may be harmful to us. We heard the true story of an evangelist who had been mightily used of God, until one evening the power and glory of God lifted this person several feet off the ground, in full view of the congregation! The experience was so impressive, that from that night on, that particular servant of God could talk only of how some day Christians would be carried from place to place in the Spirit all over the world to proclaim the Gospel! It became that evangelist's one theme, to the serious hindrance of preaching the Gospel, and a good ministry was rendered almost useless.

It is worthwhile to stop and analyze this particular example. What was the purpose of this miracle? We might say at once: "Oh, it was to prove to the onlookers that what the evangelist was saying was true!" No, that won't quite do; because, you see, Satan can also lift people off the ground in the phenomenon called "levitation." Among those who dabble in the occult today, some are experimenting with this very thing, trying to learn how to float off the ground, or how to lift heavy objects by the aid of "spiritual" powers. So-called table tipping, a familiar party-game variety of spiritism, is a form of levitation. The fact that someone is lifted off the ground in no way proves him to be of God, any more than the fact that he might heal the sick would prove him to be of God.

In this case, there was no need of a miracle to prove that the evangelist was of God—that was clear from what was being said; the Gospel of Jesus Christ was being proclaimed. What then was the purpose of the miracle? It was simply to rejoice the heart of the people who were listening by showing again how real God is! It was just God expressing His love to the speaker and the hearers in an extraordinary way. Our evangelist friend made the mistake of getting ahead of God, and ahead of the Scriptures, in speculating about something God may perhaps do in the future, and building a doctrine on it. Though it is possible that as the battle waxes hotter there will be more instances of persons being transported in the Spirit, yet we have no scriptural precedent for saying that God is going to establish it as a "ministry." If ever anyone could have used such an "airline," it would have been St. Paul, but we have no record of his ever having been transported in this manner. Although God worked in his life through other miracles, he *traveled* the hard way!

Right after the baptism with the Holy Spirit, people experience a greater release of the miraculous in their lives. Then often comes a slackening of these experiences, because the old ways of thinking and living creep back in, and God has to enroll us in the school of the Holy Spirit. He has things to teach us before He can trust us more fully in this area, lest pride and other sins get in, causing us to exalt ourselves, and then fall with a resounding thud! (I Tim. 2:6). The wise Christian, however, once having tasted of the wondrous works of the Lord, is encouraged to yield to God's dealings and lessons so he can *go on*, and not regress into the way things were before. It is the Father's will for us to remain in this new dimension.

We have already warned in detail in a previous chapter and earlier in this chapter that for every gift of God, there will be a demonic counterfeit. A mushroom and a toadstool look almost exactly alike, but one is delicious food and the other deadly poison. Only the Scripture can teach us to detect spiritual "toadstools." God's true miracles come only through those who have received His divine Son, Jesus. Christians do not expect miracles for the sake of miracles, but because God promised that they would follow in the lives of His children, and because they meet human needs and lead others to Jesus.

The New Testament recounts more miraculous events in the life of St. Paul than in any of the original twelve apostles. If we think that the first apostles had a special "in" because they walked and talked with Jesus during His earthly life, we should be encouraged by Paul, who did not know Jesus "after the flesh" (II Cor. 5:16). Also, Paul's power in the Holy Spirit did not decrease as he grew older. We find him manifesting God's miraculous keeping and healing power more strongly, if anything, in the last chapter of Acts, than in the earlier times (Acts 27–28). Paul never slowed down even in his old age.

Many times God's miracles are done in such a "supernaturally natural" way that you may miss them if you are not on the alert! Look with expectancy for God's miracles to be manifested in you and through your life. Pray that God's power will be manifested also through the rest of the body of Christ. Expect a miracle, and keep your eyes on Jesus.

11
The Gift of Faith

The Bible talks about faith from Genesis to Revelation but there's only one definition given. It is found in the Book of Hebrews: "Now faith is the substance of things hoped for, the evidence of things not seen" (Heb. 11:1 KJV). We learn several things from this verse. Faith is *now* or it's not faith at all. Faith is present tense; hope is future tense. Faith is believing before seeing, but it will eventually bring substance to what you have believed. Faith is not passive but active.

Everyone, believers and nonbelievers alike, can understand *natural human faith*. People have faith in the things of this world through the experience of the five senses. It takes natural faith to turn on the television set, and to believe we will see and hear something of interest. Even though the average person doesn't understand the electronics of television, he still has faith enough to turn it on. It takes natural faith to sit down in a chair. If a person could see the molecular structure of that chair, and the large amount of space represented in something that looks so solid, he might sit down more gingerly! It takes natural faith to turn on a light, ride in an airplane, drive a car, and just to live! A person can have this kind of faith and not believe in God at all. Natural faith is trust in something or someone you can see, hear, or touch. "Seeing is believing."

True faith that comes from God is *super*natural, or above the natural senses. There are three kinds of supernatural faith.

The first is *"saving faith."* The Bible tells us that without faith it is impossible to please God (Heb. 11:6). Salvation does not come from our good deeds but from our faith in Jesus Christ. "Believe (have faith in) the Lord Jesus Christ and you will be saved . . ." (Acts 16:31). The key to Christian faith is not "seeing is believing," but "believing before seeing." "Faith," says the writer to the Hebrews, "is the substance of things hoped for, the evidence of things *not seen*" (Heb. 11:1). Jesus is not evident to our physical senses, but by the Holy Spirit we are able to experience His love and fellowship here and now. This saving faith itself is a gift of God, and not something we manufacture (Eph. 2:8–9). Saving faith comes to man by the proclamation of God's Word. "Faith comes by hearing, and hearing by the Word of God" (Rom. 10:17).

Once we have received Jesus, the Scripture says that each Christian has been given "the measure of faith" (Rom. 12:3). We all start out with an equal measure yet some continue to grow in faith and some don't, but the choice is ours. God always has more in store for His children; His supply is unlimited.

The second kind is faith as a *"fruit of the Spirit"* (Gal. 5:22). This comes as result of our salvation: union with Christ. Jesus says: "I am the Vine, and you are the branches. He that abideth in Me, and I in Him, the same brings forth much fruit" (John 15:5). From the time of our union with Him (the Vine) we have the potential of bearing fruit.

Our faith (trust, belief) in Jesus is the work of God the Holy Spirit, and it is He Who supplies the faith as we go along in the Christian life. Our part is to respond to Him. Faith in Jesus, both initial faith and continuing faith, is the basis for all the other fruit and gifts of the Spirit. Its importance cannot be overestimated. "According to your faith be it unto you," says Jesus; and in another place, "All things are possible to him that believes" (Matt. 9:29; Mark 9:23).

Faith the fruit is brought about through the process of time. One doesn't plant a tree, and the next day pick fruit. The tree must be cultivated, fed, and watered. The word "abide" means to take up permanent residence. The result of abiding is the fruit of a Godly Christian character. Our growth in the fruit of faith depends on a consistent walk with Jesus, daily food from the Scriptures, and fellowship in the Holy Spirit.

The *gift of faith* is potential in the believer from the time of receiving Jesus, but like the other gifts, it becomes much more active after the Baptism in the Holy Spirit. Unlike the fruit, it is given instantaneously. It is a sudden surge of faith, usually in a crisis, to confidently believe without a doubt, that as we act or speak in Jesus' Name it shall come to pass.

The word "confession" comes from the two root words in Greek, *homo logos,* which means to speak the same thing as the Word of God. The spoken gift of faith is confessing what God says, as led by the Holy Spirit. One of the best Scriptures describing this is recorded in Matthew:

"And Jesus answering saith unto them, Have faith in God." The literal translation of the Greek is: "Have the faith of God." "For verily I say unto you, that whosoever shall say unto this mountain, be thou removed, and be thou cast into the sea; and shall not doubt in his heart, but shall believe that those things which he saith shall come to pass; he shall have whatever he saith" (Mark 11:22-23).

Elijah is a stirring example of this gift in the Old Testament. He suddenly appears on the scene in I Kings 17:1 (KJV) and announces to Ahab, the most wicked king Israel ever had: "As the Lord God of Israel liveth, before Whom I stand, there shall not be dew nor rain these years, but according to my word!"

And sure enough, there wasn't! The prophet Elijah must have lived at a very high level of faith, even though we know that there were times when his faith collapsed almost completely for the time being, as in I Kings 19:3, when he just plain lost his nerve and ran away! It would seem that to meet crises such as the one we have mentioned, or the tremendous test on Mt. Carmel: "If the Lord be God, serve Him, but if Ba'al be god, serve him!" (I Kings 18:21) when the fire came down from Heaven to confirm Elijah's God as the true one to serve, there must have been mighty surges of faith, special gifts of faith.

On the other hand, an example of an acted gift of faith is found in the familiar incident in the life of the prophet Daniel. Daniel was "framed" by some jealous associates, and sentenced to be thrown into a den of hungry lions. Daniel said no word, but simply trusted God, and the lions did not hurt him. Even for as great a man as Daniel, it likely took a special surge of faith for him to go through this frightful experience (Dan. 6:17–28).

In the Lord Jesus Christ, the fruit and the gift merge completely as He was living always at the peak of the fullness of faith in His Father. The Gospels are full of examples of His great faith. One day Jesus and His disciples set out to go across the lake in a small boat. Jesus was tired, and had gone to sleep in the stern on a cushion. Suddenly a squall arose and the waves began to break over the boat, filling it with water. The disciples were terrified, and awakened Jesus. He simply spoke to the storm and it immediately quieted down. Obviously, even awakening from a sound sleep, he needed no special infusion of faith to perform the miracle. The disciples, on the other hand, failed to exercise faith but had to be reassured by a miracle (Mark 4:35–41).

The gift of faith is distinct from the working of miracles, which we have studied in the last chapter, though it may produce miracles. If the disciples in the storm-tossed boat had remained calm and assured in spite of their dangerous situation, they would

have been manifesting the gift of faith. As it was, Jesus had to
still the storm by a miracle. If Daniel in the lions' den had slain
the dangerous animals with but a gesture it would have been the
gift of miracles. As it was, he rested unharmed in the presence
of the fully active lions, showing an even greater amount of *faith*.
In the New Testament believers, we can see the same sort of
thing going on. Who was more "wobbly" than Peter? After Pentecost, the Holy Spirit steadied him down considerably, but,
just like us, he had his ups and downs! He had his eyes so much
on what people would think, that Paul had to "withstand him to
his face" (Gal. 2:11). Yet when word was brought to him that
Dorcas, or Tabitha, the beloved woman disciple in Joppa, had
died, he went without hesitation and spoke the word of faith:
"Tabitha, get up!" (Acts 9:40).

We may see the example of acted faith in Acts 12. Peter was
arrested by Herod Agrippa I and thrown into prison, with the
expressed intention that he be executed the very next morning, as
had already been done with James bar Zebedee. We read:

"Peter was sleeping between two soldiers, bound with two
chains: and the keepers before the door kept the prison. And
suddenly an angel of the Lord appeared and a light shone in the
prison; and he struck Peter on the side, and woke him, saying,
'Quick! get up!' And the chains fell off his hands." The angel
brought Peter out of the prison before he even knew that he was
awake! (Acts 12:11).

Now the word that is used for "struck" in the above passage
means a "blow," not a love pat! Peter was sleeping so soundly, that
even when he was awake, it took him a while to "come to," to
realize what had happened! This is *acted* faith, in a sense very
like Daniel's. You or I might have been lying awake worrying
about what was going to happen to us, or perhaps planning a
way to escape, but not Peter! He was sleeping soundly, leaving
it all in God's hands, and his faith was rewarded.

The Gift of Faith Today.

We've already mentioned the great events which have been taking place in Indonesia today as millions of Moslems and Communists are accepting Christ. Accompanying this revival have been miracles of New Testament magnitude. Three years ago there were already thirty-three thoroughly documented cases of the raising of the dead on the Island of Timor. When David duPlessis visited Indonesia this year he told us that when he asked how many dead had been raised to date, they replied: "We've lost count—besides no one believes us, anyway!"

A friend, Sherwin McCurdy of Dallas, Texas, was used to raise a man from the dead. The story was told in *Christian Life* magazine for October 1969.[1] McCurdy was waiting for a taxi outside the Amarillo airport early in the morning, when a frightened nine-year-old boy came running up, pleading for help: "My daddy's dying!" he gasped. Following the boy, McCurdy found a car in the ditch, the driver a man in middle years, obviously dead. An older son explained that his father had had a heart attack about forty-five minutes before. He had been giving him mouth-to-mouth resuscitation, but to no avail. The rest of the family was in near hysteria. The Lord gave a gift of faith to McCurdy, instructing him to lay hands on the corpse, commanding the spirit of death to depart, and the spirit of life to return. Sherwin did so. "It was like putting my hands on a piece of melting ice!" he said, but when he laid his palms on that cold forehead (the corpse was already rigid, and cyanotic in death), and did as God told him, the man instantly returned not only to life, but to normalcy, and he and his whole family accepted Jesus as Lord and Savior.

A dramatic and true example of the gift of faith coupled with the gift of miracles comes from an Elim missionary in Tanzania.

[1] S. W. McCurdy as told to Jamie Buckingham, "In Time for God's Appointment," *Christian Life Magazine*, October, 1969, p. 40.

A native congregation had gathered for Easter services, when suddenly an enraged lioness in a wild mood dashed out of the jungle, attacking everything in her path. She killed several domestic animals, then a woman and a child and headed directly for the assembled believers. Bud Sickler, the Elim missionary who received the report from the native pastor, says:

"The congregation suddenly saw the lioness. She had stopped only a few yards from them, snarling ferociously. The people trembled with shock! The preacher shouted, 'Don't be afraid— the God who saved Daniel from the lions is here—the risen Christ of Easter is here.' He turned to the lioness and cried, 'You, lion, I curse you in the name of Jesus Christ!'

"Then the most amazing thing happened. From the scattered clouds, without a sign of rain, a bolt of lightning struck the lioness and she dropped dead. The preacher then jumped on the carcass and used it as a platform to preach!" The final punch of the story is that not only were the people's lives saved, but the whole village was stirred, and seventeen gave their lives to the Lord Jesus! [2]

The level of faith in which we are living may ebb and flow. Sometimes we find that we are strong in faith; the Holy Spirit in our spirit is allowed to work, and wonderful things happen in our lives. At other times the "hang-ups," doubts, fears, and the "debris" in our souls that the Holy Spirit is working to remove get in the way, and we are not able to function as well. Some believers consistently operate at a high level of faith while others often have difficulty "getting off the ground." Though the gift of faith may be active from time to time in our lives, it should not surprise us if we also experience times of doubt. This should only serve to remind us of the Scripture: "It is *God* who works in you both to will and to do of his good pleasure" (Phil. 2:13). Expect the

[2] *World Map Digest* (Fontana, Calif., 1970), X, 22.

Lord to manifest this wonderful gift of faith through you, just as you expect the other gifts.

* * * * *

Concluding this section on the gifts of power, we note again that the gifts of the Holy Spirit are often manifested together, interacting with, and enhancing one another.

In the Gospel of Matthew, Jesus gave His apostles this commission: "Heal the sick, cleanse the lepers, raise the dead, cast out devils: freely you have received, freely give" (Matt. 10:8). In order to carry out this command, all three gifts of power would be required: heal the sick and cleanse the lepers (gifts of healing), raise the dead (gifts of faith, miracles, and healing), and cast out demons (gift of faith, plus others in our next section).

12
Discerning of Spirits

We call the last three gifts *revelation gifts* because they consist of information supernaturally revealed from God. We might call them simply the "mind of Christ being manifested through a Spirit-filled believer." Each of these gifts is the God-given ability to receive from Him facts concerning something, anything, about which it is humanly impossible for us to know, revealed to the believer so that he may be protected, pray more effectively, or help someone in need.[1]

Discernment

Before we talk about spiritual discernment we need to discuss discernment in general. First there is what we may call *"natural discernment"* which Christian and non-Christian alike have. This

---

[1] There are only two ways by which the human mind can receive information other than through the physical senses of seeing, hearing, smelling, tasting, feeling. One is by opening the mind to the "psychic" world, so that information is received directly into the mind from the spirits of Satan. This is what happens in the phenomena of so-called ESP, spiritism, clairvoyance, etc. It is, as we have said previously, totally forbidden by God, and no one should engage in it.

The other way is for information to come to the mind from the renewed spirit, in turn inspired and informed by the Holy Spirit. This kind of supernatural knowledge is acceptable to God—it comes directly from Him—and is safe for us. The Holy Spirit is going to share with us only those

is the judgment that we pass on people and circumstances, and on our own behavior, and is derived from teachings received in our homes, and the effect of our environment and culture. Our natural "consciences" are composed of this kind of material, and therefore are very unreliable. The mind, and that part of it called the conscience, is a mixture of good and evil, truth and error. Its discernment and moral judgments have no absolute value. It is a truism that standards of human morality vary from culture to culture, and from generation to generation, and all the natural mind can tell is what agrees with or is acceptable or unacceptable to the time and place in which we are living. This is what the world in general uses as a basis for decisions. There is no stability in it.

True intellectual discernment comes not from the fallen natural mind but from the mind that is being renewed in Christ. This discernment grows as we meet and receive Christ and get to know Him better, through fellowship and through the study of the Word of God. As the Book of Hebrews tells us: "Every one that uses milk is unskillful in the word of righteousness, for he is a babe. But strong meat belongs to them that are of full age, even those who by reason of use have their senses (Greek: *perceptions, judgment*) exercised to *discern* both good and evil" (Heb. 5:13-14). As we grow in the Christian life, the Holy Spirit sorts through our minds and consciences, discarding the wrong, and adding what is right. If God has been permitted to work in this way, as time goes on, our minds and consciences will become more and more in agreement with the Scriptures and with the Holy Spirit living in us. We become so imbued with the "flavor" of what Jesus Christ is like, and how God works, that we immediately recognize *intellectually* something that is

---

things that He knows to be needful for us, and helpful to us and others. We receive this knowledge, not through trying to develop some mysterious occult ability, but by living close to God in Jesus Christ, and allowing His Spirit to work in our lives.

different. It is very important for believers to develop this kind of discernment. It is a strong defense against false doctrine. We should be able to say immediately: "That doesn't sound like God! God doesn't *act* that way!" if we hear a strange new teaching that is not in keeping with the truth.

Our own behavior toward God and our fellowman will of course be affected by our growth in intellectual discernment. Before Paul accepted Jesus personally, he thought it a matter of good conscience to persecute Christians. After his conversion, and after many years of walking with the Lord, Paul says:

"I have lived in all good conscience before God until this day" (Acts 23:1 KJV). "I do my utmost always to have a clear conscience before God and toward men" (Acts 24:16). We should pray that our minds and consciences will be so renewed by the Spirit that we can say this too.

False Supernatural Discernment

A young woman from St. Luke's Church was going along the street in downtown Seattle one day, minding her own business, when suddenly an elderly lady rushed at her, screaming obscenities and threats, and waving her stick angrily. The Christian girl was startled, but not frightened, as she recognized what was happening. The old woman was demonically possessed and the evil spirit in her detected the presence of the Holy Spirit in the young lady, and immediately was aroused to angry protest.

Such incidents are not uncommon, although not usually as dramatic and unexpected as this one. If a person has been serving Satan, and gotten himself thoroughly oppressed or possessed by enemy power and influence, he will be repelled by the presence of anyone who is walking in the Spirit. This is the devil's counterfeit of the discerning of spirits.

One of the most striking examples of this is the great resentment shown by spiritualists to those who have received the baptism in the Holy Spirit. Dennis was sitting at the head table at a Full Gospel Businessmen's banquet one day, when the man next to him, a well-known physician who had received the Holy Spirit, showed him a letter from an acquaintance scurrilously and savagely attacking and condemning the good doctor for his Pentecostal activities. Dennis said:

"That man is a spiritualist, isn't he?"

The doctor nodded: "I'm afraid he is," he concurred.

Do not be surprised if you receive attack and persecution out of all proportion from associates who not only do not know the Lord but are actively engaged in unscriptural and forbidden practices.

Discerning of Spirits

We come now to the spiritual gift. Like all of the gifts this does not come through training but is given in a moment when and as it is needed. Any Christian may manifest this gift, but like the others, it is intensified after the baptism in the Holy Spirit. Believers who have not been baptized in the Spirit are not likely to be aware enough of the activities of Satan to be concerned about discerning of spirits, although of course, there are exceptions.

By the gift of discerning of spirits the believer is enabled to know immediately what is motivating a person or situation. A believer may be operating under the inspiration of the Holy Spirit, he may be expressing his own thoughts, feelings, and desires from his soul, it is even possible that he may be allowing an alien spirit to oppress him, and be bringing thoughts from that wrong spirit. An unbeliever, of course, may be completely possessed by the wrong spirit. The gift of discerning of spirits immediately reveals what is taking place.

It may help us to understand the gift of discerning of spirits if we recognize what it is like to discern the Holy Spirit. The gospel song says: "There's a sweet, sweet Spirit in this place and I know that It's the Spirit of the Lord!" Believers know that joyful sense of, or witness to, the presence of the Holy Spirit in another person, or in a meeting. When we say: "I really felt the presence of God," we are speaking of the discerning of the Holy Spirit. We experienced a rather amusing example of this kind of discernment after we came to Seattle.

Dennis had been invited to attend a choir concert in a nearby church. The choral director was a baptized-in-the-Holy-Spirit Christian, who had many friends at St. Luke's. Dennis knew that some twenty or thirty of the people from the church who had received the Holy Spirit were planning to go to the concert, too. He arrived a little late, and was seated in the balcony. He was surprised, at looking over the congregation on the main floor, to see no sign of any of his friends. Dennis enjoyed the program, but all the way through he was puzzled by a little inner "lift" of joy, a definite witness of the Holy Spirit that kept "nudging" him all the way through the concert. It was great, but he couldn't understand what it meant. The choir was good, but not *that* good! The explanation came as he left the church at the end of the evening, when he was greeted by some thirty "Spirit-filled" Episcopalians who had been sitting right under him—right beneath the balcony. They were out of sight, but Dennis' spirit had discerned their presence!

Reports from those who work behind the Iron Curtain reveal that this gift becomes very important as persecution increases. There are many cases of Christian recognizing Christian, each "in the Spirit" without having to use words. In one place, Christian meetings were continuously being interfered with, so the brethren simply stopped announcing any time or place for their fellowship, but depended upon the Holy Spirit to tell those who should be there! Everyone was present and accounted for just the same. This was probably a combination of the gift of knowledge and the gift of discernment.

We may understand the discerning of wrong spirits by seeing it as the opposite of all this. The sense of the presence of the Holy Spirit brings joy and love and peace; the discerning of wrong spirits brings a sense of heaviness and unrest.

Some years ago, when we were very "green" in all these matters, a person visited St. Luke's Church and spoke to our local prayer meeting. He came with good recommendations, and seemed to be "on the level." Says Dennis: "I had handed over the meeting to our visitor, and he seemed to me to be saying acceptable things, yet as I looked at the faces of the listeners it was obvious that something was wrong. They looked distressed, unhappy, uncomfortable. One woman even got up from her place and left the room, excusing herself as she passed by me by saying that she felt nauseated. I did not have the sense to stop the speaker and say: 'Excuse me, but you are making the people feel sick—what is wrong?' The man went on his way the next day to another town, but as he spoke there, the chairman stopped him and said: 'Your words are fine, but I discern a wrong spirit in your life.[2] What is it?' The man, thus challenged, confessed that he was an impostor, living in open sin." Obviously the purpose of such a gift was not only to protect the people from the enemy's deception, but also to bring this man to repentance and deliverance.

Sometimes the disturbing influence will not be from the person who is speaking or ministering, but from one who is simply present in the meeting. An individual who is actively engaged in something like spiritism can throw a coldness over a Holy Spirit prayer meeting just by his presence. If there seems to be a dead-

[2] Please note that "wrong spirits" are not, and cannot be, the spirits of people who have died. Discerning of spirits has nothing to do with spiritism or spiritualism. The spirits of departed human beings are *not* on this earth, and to attempt to contact them is forbidden! The "wrong spirits" we are talking about are spoken of in the Scriptures as "the rulers of the darkness of this world," that is, fallen angels or else "demons" (Eph. 6:12, Matt. 10:8).

ness in the meeting, it is well to stop and pray that the Spirit will reveal the trouble. If there is someone present who is under oppression he may be helped and delivered.

Thus discerning of spirits is a kind of "police" gift, to keep the enemy's influence from causing serious problems in the fellowship. Unfortunately when people receive this kind of discernment, they often hesitate to use it for fear of seeming hard or unloving. If you have spiritual discernment that something is wrong in a meeting, and you are not the leader, quietly and as unobtrusively as possible let the leader know, so that there can be prayer for the gifts of knowledge from the Lord to show what is wrong, and wisdom to know how it should be dealt with. There will probably be others with the same discernment, as it is usually given to more than one—for confirmation.

Discerning of spirits is especially needful when the other gifts are exercised in a meeting. We are not expected to accept every word spoken through the gifts of utterance, nor in any other manifestation or even in preaching, but we are only to accept what is quickened to us by the Holy Spirit and is in agreement with the Bible. "Let the prophets speak two or three, and let the other judge (discern)" (I Cor. 14:29 KJV). The gifts of the Holy Spirit are pure, but the channels they come through are at varying degrees of yieldedness and sanctification. One manifestation may be seventy-five percent God, but twenty-five percent the person's own thoughts. We must discern between the two.

Then too, the enemy may send people into a meeting expressly to disturb it with counterfeit manifestations. In Acts 16 a woman possessed with a spirit of divination, for several days continued to interrupt Paul with a word which sounded something like prophecy: "These men are the servants of the most high God, which show us the way of salvation" (Acts 16:17). What she was saying was true enough, but she was speaking under the influence of the enemy. When Paul discerned this wrong spirit the Scripture says he was grieved within; he then commanded the evil spirit to leave her and she was set free. This example shows that counterfeit manifestations should be dealt with, if possible, at the time they happen.

The story of Elisha and his servant Gehazi is an Old Testament example of the gifts of discerning of spirits and knowledge. Naaman, a captain in the Syrian army, was a leper. In obedience to the prophet Elisha's instructions he washed in Jordan seven times and was healed. Naaman offered Elisha gifts to show his gratitude but Elisha would not accept them. Elisha's servant Gehazi, however, secretly followed Naaman, and lied to him, telling him that Elisha had just received two unexpected guests, and would Naaman please give two changes of clothing and some money—all of which Gehazi, of course, kept for himself. When Gehazi returned to his master, Elisha discerned his dishonest spirit and then knew by the gift of knowledge exactly what had been done (II Kings 5).

There are many examples of Jesus' discerning spirits. He had not previously met Nathanael, but discerned immediately that he was "an Israelite indeed, in whom is no guile" (John 1:47 KJV). When Peter made his great confession about Jesus: "Thou art the Christ, the Son of the living God!" Jesus commended him. When Jesus began to tell His followers, however, that He was to die, Peter would not accept His words. He began to rebuke Jesus, saying, "Be it far from thee, Lord: this shall not be unto thee!" Jesus discerned that Peter was speaking in a wrong spirit, and said: "Get thee behind me, Satan: you are an offense to me: for you savor not the things that be of God, but those that be of men" (Matt. 16:15–23). When Jesus was not received in the village of the Samaritans, James and John were so angry that they asked Jesus whether they should command fire to come down from heaven and consume the people. But Jesus said: "You know not what manner of spirit you are of" (Luke 9:54–55). We see by these last two examples, that even close followers of Jesus can be temporarily misled.

Fulfilled prophecy and other Biblical signs indicate that we may be living in the final part of the Last Days. Scripture teaches that before Jesus Christ returns to earth, there will be many more deceiving spirits unleashed, so to be able to discern between the counterfeit and the true will be increasingly needful (Matt. 24; Rev. 13:11–14).

Another important use of the gift of discerning of spirits is in bringing deliverance[3] to those bound by the enemy. One of the first signs that Jesus said would follow believers is that they would cast out demons in His (Jesus') Name. About twenty-five percent of Jesus' ministry was spent in delivering captives from Satan, and we too should expect to be used in this way. Jesus said: "The Spirit of the Lord God is upon me; because the Lord has anointed me to preach good tidings unto the meek; he has sent me to bind up the brokenhearted, to proclaim liberty to the captives, and the opening of the prison to them that are bound . . ." (Isa. 61:1). In this Scripture Isaiah was speaking specifically of Jesus, but now since Calvary, with Christ living in us, we too are anointed with the Holy Spirit, and it also applies to us. This does not mean we are to go and look specifically for those in need of deliverance or to develop an unhealthy fascination with the subject, but we do need to know how to pray for people with such needs. If we are yielded to God and properly prepared, He will bring those in need of deliverance across our pathway.

The Epistle of James tells us how to prepare to pray for those who need to be set free: "Submit yourselves therefore to God. Resist the devil, and he will flee from you" (Jas. 4:7 KJV). The first step then is to "submit yourself to God." You may do this by praying, and asking Him to show areas in your own life that need correction. All known sin must be dealt with, and made right.

---

[3] Exorcism is the ancient name used for this kind of ministry of casting out evil spirits.

It is also important to establish yourself in the authority you have in Jesus by studying the Scriptures on this subject.[4] Realize that through the Name of Jesus you have authority to bind evil spirits and cast them out. Some people have been taught that in dealing with an evil spirit one must say, "The Lord rebuke you," instead of confronting the enemy directly. They quote Jude 9 and Zechariah 3:2 where an angel dealing with Satan says, "The Lord rebuke you." Holy angels, though sinless creatures of God, must deal with the enemy in this way. However, we Christians are not only creatures of God but *children* of God, with Christ in us. Jesus told us to deal with the enemy directly: ". . . In my name shall *they* cast out devils . . ." (Mark 16:17 KJV),[5] and throughout the New Testament it is never done in any other way.

Unless the person with whom you are praying is a close friend or relative, *always* have a third person with you when praying for deliverance. This third person may just be sitting or kneeling and agreeing in prayer. If the person needing deliverance wants to talk confidentially, the third person can retire into the next room while you talk, but always have him present when any deliverance prayers are said. It is not wise for a man to pray in private for deliverance for a woman, or *vice versa* (it is always better for the same sexes to minister to each other, in all areas of ministry). If it is inevitable that a man should be praying for deliverance for a woman or girl, be sure that another *woman* is present.

A Christian cannot be possessed in his spirit (where the Holy Spirit dwells), but his mind, emotions, or will (the three parts of the soul) may be depressed, oppressed, obsessed, or even possessed if he has let the enemy in by choosing to walk in known sin rather than with the Lord Jesus. A non-Christian, of course, may be possessed, spirit, soul, and body. It follows, then, that

[4] See Eph. 1:1–23; 2:1–10; Luke 10:19; Gal. 2:20; II Cor. 5:17; I John 4:4.
[5] See also II Cor. 10:4–5.

the most important first step in helping a person to be delivered from the enemy is to make sure that he or she knows the Lord Jesus as Savior.

If the person you are ministering to is not a Christian, lead Him to accept Jesus. We suggest a re-reading of chapter one to help you at this point. You may find it a great help to have a definite "plan of salvation" in mind, with appropriate Scriptures. A typical series might be:

1. Rom. 3:23: "For all have sinned, and come short of the glory of God."
2. Rom. 6:23a: "For the wages of sin is death."
3. Rom. 5:8: "But God commendeth His love toward us, in that, while we were yet sinners, Christ died for us."
4. Rom. 6:23b: "But the gift of God is eternal life through Jesus Christ our Lord."
5. John 1:12: "But as many as received Him, to them gave He power to become the sons of God, even to them that believe on His Name."
6. Rev. 3:20: "Behold, I stand at the door, and knock; if any man hear my voice, and open the door, I will come in to him, and will sup with him, and he with me."

Read these verses and explain them, and then lead the person to pray a prayer such as the one given at the end of the first chapter of this book—or a similar prayer in his own words.

Now that you are both Christians, and protected by the Blood of Jesus, make an open confession of this: "Thank you, Jesus, for the protection of Your precious Blood, over us and around us." Ask the person you are praying with if he feels assured that God has forgiven him his sins. If he has any doubt about it, emphasize the Scripture to him: "If we confess our sins, He is faithful and just to forgive us our sins, and to cleanse us from all unrighteousness" (I John 1:9 KJV). It may help for him to confess his sins to God in your hearing and presence.[6] If so, listen quietly and prayerfully to what he has to say, and when he is finished, declare God's forgiveness to him. Say something like this:

"I have heard you confess your sins to God, and I know you are truly repentant. God says: 'As far as the east is from the west, so far have I removed your sin from you'" (Ps. 103:12). If the person still has difficulty, you may need to call on a trained pastor to give further counsel in order to convince him, and set his mind at rest.

Be sure, of course, that you have confessed and asked forgiveness for known sin in your own life, and that you have forgiven others. A Christian should daily be living in this state of forgiveness and forgivenness.

Try, if possible, to find out the exact nature of the spirit or spirits you are dealing with. Let the Holy Spirit lead you in this, as in everything else. Don't get into an interminable "counseling" session, which can waste much time, but do try to find out what kind of thing is troubling the person: is it fear, hate, lust, perverse ideas, feelings of persecution, fear of animals, anger, etc.? Now have the person name the things that are troubling him. Treat each problem as a spiritual entity, and *address it directly* as such. The devil is very clever at this point, and he will try to get the person to pray like this: "I cast out this anxiety neurosis!" or "I rebuke this spirit of anxiety." No. Have him say rather: "Spirit of Anxiety, I bind you in the Name of Jesus, under His precious Blood, and cast you into outer darkness, never to return, in Jesus' Name!" You may need to have him or her repeat this prayer (a phrase at a time) after you at first, but then

---

[6] If you do listen to someone else's confession of sin to God, remember that you must never, under any circumstances, reveal what you have heard to anyone—not even to your closest and dearest friend. You must forget what you have heard. It is a very serious sin to willfully reveal what has been told you in the confidence of a person confessing his sin to God.

try to get the person to say the prayer himself. After he has said it, you repeat it, rebuking and casting out the spirit from him, agreeing with him in the prayer. It is important to have the person in need of deliverance learn to pray his own prayer, as in this way he gains confidence in using his authority over the enemy, and can pray for himself, if the enemy seeks to return.

You will find that as the person gets the idea, he will often continue to pray for other problems which were not named at first, as the Holy Spirit brings them to mind. Some spirits may create more emotional reaction in the oppressed person than others. Some may create nausea, or exaggerated coughing, yawning, sneezing, etc. There may from time to time be a more violent reaction, even to being thrown down on the floor. If such things happen, don't allow yourself or the other persons to be put off by them. Praise the Lord, claim the protection of Jesus' Blood, and go on! On the other hand, don't feel that because such reactions *don't* take place, nothing has happened! Do not think, either, that the fact that a person has a physical reaction means that he has been delivered! These manifestations are side effects of the deliverance.

If the person needing prayer is unable to cooperate, or has no insight into his problems, you alone will need to bind the spirits and cast them out in the Name of Jesus and under His Blood just as the Apostle Paul did in Acts 16: 16–18. If on the other hand a person is perfectly in control of his senses and willpower and does not want help, you are probably wasting your time ministering to him, until he himself wants help and asks for it. Some people really enjoy their problems! Through them, Satan delights in wasting the time and energy of Christians!

In praying for deliverance you may have to be very forceful. The spirit *must* obey you when you command it by faith, in the Name of Jesus. If the spirit detects any hesitancy on your part, it will evade your command. Insist! (It is well to explain quickly and simply to the "patient" that you are not talking to him when you are rebuking the evil spirit. Just say something like: "I'm not talking to you, but to the spirit that is troubling you.")

There is no example in Scripture of the laying on of hands for casting out spirits, and most agree that it should not be done. We don't believe the person ministering, if he is a Christian, and protected by the Blood of Christ, can be harmed, but the person in need of deliverance will often react strongly and even violently to being touched. It is better to avoid physical contact while offering prayer for deliverance.

When the deliverance has been accomplished, praise the Lord and give Him glory! *Now* lay your hands on the person's head and pray that every empty place left by the spirits that have been driven out will be filled with the Holy Spirit. If the person has not been baptized in the Holy Spirit, this is an excellent time to explain to him how to receive, and to help him receive. It is imperative that his house be filled to overflowing with the Holy Spirit and His power.

Emphasize to the person the importance of daily feeding on the Word of God, prayer, praise, and fellowship with others in the Lord. The last chapter of this book, entitled "The Narrow Way," will provide detailed suggestions in this area.

These are only some brief guidelines, but before leaving the subject, let us point out that this casting out of spirits is by no means limited to those who are seriously and deeply oppressed or possessed. Any time you feel that a spirit from the enemy is harrassing you and you cannot seem to get freedom through your own prayers, never hesitate to call on a friend in the Lord to pray with you and agree to cast out the evil. Any time you are having a struggle with a besetting sin—anger, lust, fear—even though it is only a mild problem, if you can't get it under control, treat it as an oppressing spirit, bind it and cast it out; and if you can't get real freedom by yourself, call for help! It may be advisable to have a qualified Christian counselor talk and pray with you.

Let us pray that our discernment of the work of the enemy in our own and other's lives will be quickened, so that we may see the captives set completely free. Let us remember, too, that after Jesus gave seventy of His followers power over the enemy and sent them out, they returned with joy, saying that the devils were subject to them through Jesus' Name. But Jesus, Who was obviously rejoicing along with them, still brought them back into perspective: "Rejoice not, that the spirits are subject unto you; but rather rejoice, because your names are written in heaven." As we pray for people to be set free from bondage, let us remember to rejoice most of all that our names are written in the Lamb's Book of Life!

13
The "Word of Knowledge" and the "Word of Wisdom"

The eighth gift in our study is the *"word of knowledge."* It is the supernatural revelation of facts past, present, or future which were *not learned through the efforts of the natural mind.* It may be described as the Mind of Christ being manifested to the mind of the believer, and is given when needed in a flash of time (I Cor. 2:16). This gift is used to protect the Christian, to show how to pray more effectively, or to show him how to help others.

The ninth gift, the *"word of wisdom,"* is the supernatural application of knowledge. It is knowing what to do with the natural or supernatural knowledge God has given you—proper judgment for action. The "word of knowledge" is supernaturally revealed information, but the "word of wisdom" tells how to *apply* the information.

The "word of wisdom" is usually given with the "word of knowledge." It is well patiently to wait for it, and not rush off "half-cocked" if you receive supernatural knowledge. Wait until God tells you what to do with it! The "word of wisdom" will show how to do what God has shown you needs doing, how to solve problems that arise, or what and how to speak in a given situation, especially when challenged about your faith. The gifts of the "word of knowledge," and "word of wisdom," may be manifested through a sudden inspiration which remains with you, a knowing deep within your spirit, through the interpretation of a dream,[1] vision, or parable, through the vocal gifts of the Holy Spirit, and though rare, may come through hearing the audible Voice of God, or an angelic visitation.

The Authorized Version of the Scripture speaks of "word" of knowledge and "word" of wisdom. "Word" translated from the Greek in both cases is λόγος (logos), which can mean "word," "matter," or "concern," and is not confined just to a spoken word. This is to say that if the gifts of knowledge or wisdom are received, whether they are spoken aloud or not, they are still the gifts of "*word* of knowledge" or "*word* of wisdom." They are not necessarily vocal gifts. These gifts are often referred to as "the word of knowledge," or "the word of wisdom." The Greek, however, does not use any article, but simply calls them "word of wisdom" and "word of knowledge." To supply any article subtly changes the meaning. We do not even have the right to use the indefinite article: "a word of knowledge," as some modern versions do, for here again the meaning is subtly changed. Nevertheless, to read smoothly in English, we have mostly used the definite article (as the Authorized and Revised Standard Versions, and the New English Bible do), but have put it outside the quotation marks, so as to show that the article refers to the gift in general, and not to the specific "word." Perhaps the absence of the article

---

[1] Although God sometimes chooses to speak to a person through a dream, this does not mean that one should keep a diary of every dream! The psychologist may be interested in dream data as a clue to what is going on in the subconscious, but this has little to do with our present topic. Many dreams are just a result of eating too much before going to bed! Some dreams are purely from the enemy; why waste your time paying attention to the confusion he has to bring? If God has spoken to you in a dream, and He wants you to recall it, you *will!* He says that the Holy Spirit will: "Bring all things to your remembrance, whatsoever I have said unto you" (John 14:26 KJV).

in the Greek is to remind us that these "words" are only fragments of God's wisdom and knowledge.

We May Distinguish Four Kinds of Knowledge:

First: Natural human knowledge which certainly is on the increase. The Book of Daniel says of the end times: ". . . Many shall run to and fro, and knowledge shall be increased (Dan. 12:4 KJV). Just recently a college professor friend stated, for example, that the increase of knowledge in the area of higher mathematics is so great that in some instances researchers in two different math fields cannot even communicate with one another. Electronic brains or computers have become a necessity in an attempt to relate and process the tremendous stockpile of facts, since it has gone beyond the human mind to do so in any reasonable length of time. As important as the knowledge of this world is, yet it often creates so much pride that some people are kept from entering into the knowledge of the Lord. The Epistle to the Corinthians says: "But the natural man receiveth not the things of the Spirit of God: for they are foolishness unto him: neither can he know them, because they are spiritually discerned" (I Cor. 2:14 KJV). Again the Scripture says: "Knowledge puffeth up, but love edifieth" (I Cor. 8:1).

Second: This fallen world's supernatural knowledge which we have mentioned previously is the natural mind's attempt to gain information by supernatural means other than through the Holy Spirit. It includes the occult, the psychic, and the "metaphysical" investigations which Satan is using to ensnare an increasing number of people today. So-called religious experiences through drugs, cults, psychic, and occult phenomena are growing in numbers—all one has to do is look at the latest books on public display to see the level of interest in such things. The fallen knowledge of this world is outside the limit of God's permission. Do not touch it!

Our third category is true intellectual knowledge, which comes by knowing God personally through Jesus Christ (John 17:3; Phil. 3:10), being filled with the Holy Spirit, and through studying the Word of God, which brings the knowledge of God's will and His ways, for which there is no substitute (Ps. 103:7; Exod. 33:13). With the natural knowledge of this world so intriguing and so much on the increase, it is even more exciting to realize that the knowledge of the Lord is increasing in His people as never before. Isaiah tells us that ". . . The earth shall be full of the knowledge of the LORD, as the waters cover the sea" (Isa. 11:9 KJV). Even the Book of Daniel and the companion Book of Revelation have been sealed up from man's full understanding until the time of the end (Dan. 12:4, 9). There is much in God's Word which is ready to be revealed to us in the last times. What glorious days we live in! Man's knowledge will pass away, but the Knowledge of the Lord is permanent and will last through Eternity (Matt. 24:35–36; I Pet. 1:25).

The fourth is the gift of "word of knowledge." In looking at this gift, let us first say what it is *not*. It is not a psychic phenomenon or extrasensory perception such as telepathy (the supposed ability to read minds), clairvoyance (the supposed ability to know things that are happening elsewhere), or precognition (the supposed ability to know the future). These "abilities" are forbidden in God's Word (I Chron. 10:13; Deut. 18:9–12). We are not to reach out for such things—or we will open the door to Satan. All activities of this nature are dangerous and wrong. Experimentation with such psychic phenomena is toying with the *fallen powers of this world* which are controlled by Satan. There are two sources of spiritual power in the world: God and Satan. Just because something is "supernatural" does not mean that it is good, or from God.

The gift of the "word of knowledge" is not a human "ability" at all, but the sheer gift of God. It is not "developed" as the demonic manifestations may be, but is manifested as a result of staying close to the Lord. The Christian has something infinitely better than the counterfeit gifts of this world, for he is tasting the *powers of the world to come*, through Jesus, and the gifts of the Holy Spirit (Heb. 6:5). The Epistle of James says: "Every good gift and every perfect gift is *from above*, and *comes down* from the Father . . ." (Jas. 1:17). God's gifts are from above, from heavenly places in Christ Jesus, where the Christian lives in His Spirit. Paul says to the Ephesians: God "hath raised us up together, and made us sit together in heavenly places in Christ Jesus . . ." (Eph. 2:6 KJV). The Christian should not use the terminology of the world to describe supernatural experiences. If a believer suddenly became aware, without receiving the knowledge through any natural channels, that a friend was in trouble, and needed his prayers and help, that would not be "extrasensory perception," but rather God manifesting the gift of the "word of knowledge." The gifts of the Holy Spirit come from and through the Holy Spirit to our *spirit,* and not from or through the soul or physical senses.

Paul says to the Christians at Corinth: "But the manifestation of the Spirit is given to every man *to profit* withal" (I Cor. 12:7 KJV). These gifts are given to profit and benefit one another. They must not be misused. When God chooses to share His knowledge with us, it is for a purpose. It is not given just to make us feel "spiritual," or clever!

Some examples of a "word of knowledge" as given in the Bible:

It was used to recover lost persons or property, as in the case of Saul and the lost donkeys (I Sam. 9:15–20; 10:21–23). (Note that the "word of knowledge" can give information in seemingly very prosaic matters. God is concerned about every human need.)

A "word of knowledge" was given to Nathan regarding the affair between King David and Bathsheba. Nathan was also given wisdom to deal with the King (II Sam. 12:7–13).

It was used to expose a hypocrite, Gehazi (II Kings 5:20–27).

Elisha, by miraculous revelation, knew the location of the Syrian army camp, thereby saving Israel from battle (II Kings 6:8–23).

The Lord Jesus used the gift of the "word of knowledge." When He laid aside his glory, He accepted the limitations of a human intellect. While on earth He was not omniscient—"all-knowing" —but all the knowledge He needed to meet any given situation was available to Him through the Holy Spirit, just as, in Him, such knowledge is available to us today.

When Jesus healed the man sick of the palsy, he also forgave his sins. This made the scribes think evil in their hearts against Him. Jesus knew by a "word of knowledge" (not by "mind reading") the condition of their hearts and openly said so (Matt. 9:2–6).

By this gift of revelation (not by "clairvoyance") Jesus "saw" Nathanael long before He met him, standing under the fig tree, and Jesus also knew what kind of person he was. We see that "word of knowledge" may reveal the whereabouts of a man and the nature of his heart or thoughts (John 1:47–50).

It was used to convince the woman at the well of her sin, and of the need to accept Jesus as Messiah. "Come see a man, which told me all things that ever I did . . ." (John 4:17–18, 29 KJV).

We see the continuing manifestation of this supernatural knowledge in the days of the early Church.

It was used to reveal corruption in the Church—Ananias and Sapphira (Acts 5:3).

A different Ananias, an otherwise unknown Christian, received in a vision the knowledge of Saul's conversion, the name of the street (Straight), and the name of the man in whose house he was staying (Judas), whom he was to look for (Saul of Tarsus), what Saul was doing (praying), his attitude (he was repentant), and his needs (healing and the baptism with the Holy Spirit) (Acts 9:11–12, 17).

The Holy Spirit revealed to Peter by the "word of knowledge" that three men were at the gate of his house in Joppa looking for him, and that he was to go with them without having any doubts (Acts 10:17–23).

For a present-day example, we'll share something that happened in Spokane, while Rita was teaching a class on the gifts of the Holy Spirit. They were not only studying this subject intellectually, but praying and expecting that the gifts would be manifested. Faith grows by hearing God's Word, and as the class studied the Scriptures the atmosphere of faith increased to a point in which the miraculous could happen. At the end of the class, as they prayed, Rita had a strong impression, an unusual feeling in her right ear. Not knowing at first where the impression was coming from she asked God's protection. Then the thought came to her, "Maybe God is trying to show me that someone here has something wrong with his right ear!" Being among friends, she decided to ask. A young woman named Fran responded immediately, and said she had been deaf in her right ear for over twenty years. Of late her deafness had begun to trouble her so much, that she had been praying earnestly for God to heal her. "The 'word of knowledge' had never come to me in this way before," said Rita, "and I knew without a doubt that God was going to heal her." The prayer group gathered around as they laid hands on Fran, but petitionary prayer wasn't necessary, for God had already revealed what He was going to do; in simple faith Rita commanded Fran's ear to be healed in Jesus' Name. Fran said that she knew something happened, but did not fully testify to her healing until she had been examined by her doctor. Later she said that when she was prayed for, her ear "popped," and her hearing was restored. The doctor confirmed that the ear had been completely healed. It has remained so ever since. This account shows a combination of three gifts beginning with a "word of knowledge," which brought a gift of faith, which in turn brought a gift of healing.

As wonderful as it is to have God speak and tell us what He is going to do and what part we will play in His plans (knowledge), yet it is equally important to have Him show us how to do our tasks (wisdom). If a mother showed and instructed a child about all the ingredients and measurements that go into making a cake, but didn't share wisdom as to how they were to be put together—the knowledge would be to no avail. In fact, the result would be a mess. So we see that knowledge and wisdom are companion gifts; it is important to have both. The Book of Proverbs tells us: "The tongue of the wise useth knowledge aright" (Prov. 15:2 KJV).

We May Also See Four Kinds of Wisdom

Natural human wisdom is naturally applied knowledge. This kind of wisdom is obviously on the increase, since knowledge is so much on the increase. Knowledge without wisdom would be futile. Of course, compared to God's wisdom, man's wisdom is but foolishness. It may also be a stumbling block to keep man from God. The wisdom of the natural man will one day pass away: "For it is written, I will destroy the wisdom of the wise, and will bring to nothing the understanding of the prudent" (I Cor. 1:19 KJV).

This fallen world's supernatural wisdom and knowledge were the very things which were used to tempt the first man and woman to disobey God's commandment. "A tree to be desired to make one *wise*," we read (Gen. 3:6 KJV). This kind of wisdom was, and continues to be, forbidden by God. Man already had natural wisdom, which was good, but now he opened himself up to supernatural evil knowledge, and the application of it, evil wisdom, which until then existed only among the fallen angels. Astrology is an example of counterfeit wisdom today (Dan. 2:27–28).

True intellectual wisdom. The Books of Proverbs and King Solomon's wisdom are good examples of this. We are told to get this kind of wisdom. It comes by respecting the Lord and the Word of God (Job 28:28; Prov. 9:10), and also by studying

God's Word which can be understood only as it is revealed by the Holy Spirit. In order to do this we must first receive Jesus Christ, Who is the wisdom of God (I Cor. 1:24), and obviously, it is important to have received the baptism with the Holy Spirit.

The Scripture says: "If any of you lack wisdom, let him ask of God, that giveth to all men liberally, and upbraideth not; and it shall be given him" (Jas. 1:5 KJV). Paul also prayed without ceasing for the Church that: "You might be filled with the knowledge of his will in all wisdom and spiritual understanding" (Col. 1:9). We should ask and believe that God will give us liberally the wisdom needed to do the best job possible for Him.

The supernatural gift of the "word of wisdom" is the sudden and miraculous giving of wisdom to meet a particular situation, or answer a particular question, or utilize a particular piece of knowledge, natural or supernatural. Like the "word of knowledge" it is not a human ability at all, but the sheer gift of God. It would be difficult to say whether wisdom or knowledge is the more important. It would be rather like trying to decide which is the more important, the paint, or the painter, for whereas the artist can't paint a picture without the materials, the materials without the person who knows how to use them can be a source of damage and ugliness. So if a person has knowledge—either in the natural or the supernatural—and has no wisdom to use it properly, much damage may be done.

Let us look at some examples of the gift of the "word of wisdom" in the Old Testament Scripture:

When Joseph interpreted Pharaoh's dream, this was not natural wisdom, or wisdom through study and preparation, but Joseph was given an immediate supernatural answer. Joseph was "on the spot"! He had been let out of prison just long enough to be given a chance to interpret this dream. Later, Joseph gave wise counsel in such matters as: the need of appointing a wise leader and officers, and how to store the needed food for the time of famine. This latter, however, was not by a "word of wisdom," but by the true intellectual wisdom that God had given Joseph, and which he used continually. This led Pharaoh to call Joseph "discreet and wise," and he placed him over all Egypt as second only to the King (Gen. 41).

God called to Moses out of a burning bush, asking him to deliver Israel from the bondage of Egypt (knowledge), and he needed the "word of wisdom" many times as he was faced with a rebellious people (Exod. 3).

God gave knowledge of the plans of construction of the Tabernacle in the Wilderness to Moses and told him that He had called Bezaleel and filled him with wisdom and knowledge (which he didn't have naturally) to work with the gold, silver, brass, stones, timber, and to do the principal work of the building of the Tabernacle (Exod. 31).

One of the great "faith" stories in the Old Testament is also a remarkable example of the Spiritual gifts of prophecy, wisdom, and knowledge. King Jehoshaphat was beset by an alliance of three powerful enemies. Knowing that he did not have the resources to defend his kingdom, he put the whole matter before the Lord. All the people of Judah "stood before the Lord," waiting for an answer. The answer came when "upon Jahaziel . . . came the Spirit of the Lord in the midst of the congregation," and Jahaziel first began to prophesy:

"Be not afraid nor dismayed by reason of this great multitude, for the battle is not yours, but God's." This was "edification, exhortation, and comfort." Then followed the "word of knowledge," as Jahaziel told the King and the people exactly where the enemy would be, and where they would find them. Again, he brought a "word of wisdom," telling them they wouldn't have to fight, but just stand still and watch what God would do. Jehoshaphat then is given a "word of wisdom" from the Lord, and instead of going out with his best warriors in the front rank, he sends out men to sing and praise the Lord—and lo and behold, the enemies proceed to ambush each other! (II Chron. 20:12-23).

Daniel had wisdom and knowledge in the intellectual realm, and therefore was chosen to teach in the King's palace. However, even greater was the supernatural word of wisdom which God gave him from time to time, so that when he was called in to Nebuchadnezzar to reveal the dream the King had forgotten and the interpretation of it (wisdom), he was able to do so. These secrets were revealed to Daniel in a "night vision." Daniel said, "Blessed be the name of God for ever and ever: for wisdom and might are His . . . He gives wisdom unto the wise, and knowledge to them that know understanding. He reveals the deep and secret things . . ." (Dan. 2:20-22). Consequently the King made Daniel ruler over Babylon and chief of the governors. In the fourth chapter of Daniel we read where Daniel again interprets Nebuchadnezzar's dream, this time telling him of the departure of his Kingdom. Later, under Belshazzar's reign, he was called in to interpret the handwriting on the wall. Daniel's life and the lives of others were spared many times through this God-given gift.

As our Example in all things, the Lord Jesus displays again and again the "word of wisdom" to meet especially challenging circumstances. The chief priests and elders of the people asked Jesus by what authority He made such great claims. Jesus' answer in the form of a question was a "word of wisdom" (Matt. 21:23-27).

The Pharisees tried to entangle Jesus in His words by asking if men should pay tribute to Caesar or not. Jesus answered with a "word of wisdom": "Render therefore unto Caesar the things which are Caesar's; and unto God the things that are God's" (Matt. 22:15-22 KJV).

A lawyer and Pharisee tempted Jesus with a question to find out which He thought was the greatest commandment in the law. Jesus answered this with wisdom. Then Jesus asked the

Pharisees, "What think ye of Christ? Whose Son is He?" When they answered, "The son of David," Jesus' reply from the Psalms was so profound that the Gospel of Matthew says from that day on they dared not ask Him any more questions (Matt. 22:34-46).

Even as Jesus had great wisdom, we are promised that in the midst of persecution He will give us "a mouth and wisdom" which our adversaries will not be able to deny or resist. This gift will be needed more in the days ahead. The Gospel of Matthew says: "But beware of men: for they will deliver you up to the councils . . . synagogues . . . governors and kings for my sake . . . But when they deliver you up, *take no thought* how or what you shall speak: for it shall be given you in that same hour what you shall speak . . ." (Matt. 10:17-19).

This passage of Scripture shows the wisdom Peter and John applied when they were threatened by the rulers of the Jews because of the healing of the lame man (Acts 4:7-21). Later when they were arrested because of this healing we read: "When they saw the boldness of Peter and John, and perceived that they were unlearned and ignorant men, they marvelled; and they took knowledge of them, that they had been with Jesus" (Acts 4:13 KJV).

It was said of those disputing with Stephen, who was a man full of faith and power: "They were not able to resist the wisdom and the spirit by which he spoke" (Acts 6:8-10).

The Apostle Paul was certainly not trained in seamanship, yet when he was involved in a shipwreck, he so took command of the situation that even though he was a prisoner being taken to Rome, the Roman officer listened to him with respect (Acts 27:21-35).

We must set our thinking aright, get rid of our old habit of limiting God in our lives, and begin to live with expectancy. In Christ are hidden "all the treasures of wisdom and knowledge" (Col. 2:3 KJV). Since Jesus Christ lives within us, the tremendous fact is that His wisdom and knowledge are there also—

ready to be revealed to us by the quickening of the Holy Spirit. With this wonderful treasure of Jesus Christ living in us, let us rest assured that the Holy Spirit will draw from the treasury that which is needed as we believe God for these gifts. Take time to thank Him right now that divine wisdom and knowledge will be manifested in your life, at God's bidding, when the need arises. Praise God for his unspeakable riches!

*   *   *

In this study of the gifts of the Spirit we began with the gifts of *inspired speech*, because they are most easily observed, and most frequently manifested; then the gifts of *power*; and lastly the gifts of *revelation*. Every supernatural happening in the Bible (excluding counterfeits, of course), can be identified with one or the other of these nine gifts of the Holy Spirit listed in I Corinthians 12:7-11.

There are three other lists in the New Testament that are termed "gifts," but one of them, in Ephesians, is a list of offices or ministries in the Church: apostles, prophets, evangelists, pastors, and teachers (Eph. 4:8, 11). In this place, too, a different word is used in the Greek: *domata*, rather than *charismata*. Another "list" is found in Romans but it is really not an attempt to list the gifts at all, but rather a series of illustrations given to instruct in Christian living (Rom. 12:4-21). It mixes a few of the gifts and ministries with other functions—some of which, according to Paul's rationale elsewhere, would be called "fruit" of the Spirit. In I Corinthians 12, the very same chapter in which the clear-cut list of the gifts appears, the Apostle again cites, at the end of the chapter, a number of the gifts and ministries for illustrative purposes.[2] It seems most in keeping with the general pattern of Scripture, though, to say that I Corinthians 12:7-11 is the list of the gifts, while Ephesians 4:11 lists the "official" min-

[2] Any of the gifts of the Spirit may develop into a ministry as we have stated before, but those at the end of this list are specifically listed as such.

istries in the Church. Similarly the fruit of the Spirit is listed in Galatians 5:22–23, but in Ephesians 5:9 (KJV), Paul uses the term in illustrative style: "The fruit of the Spirit is in all goodness and righteousness and truth."

Any person who has been baptised with the Holy Spirit may exercise any of the nine spiritual gifts as the need arises, and as the Holy Spirit chooses. We know many Christians who have during a period of years been used in all of the nine gifts of the Spirit. This doesn't mean that they're more spiritual than the rest but merely that they have been perhaps more available and expectant.

We pray that this study will help to bring greater understanding so that the gifts of power and revelation will be manifested in the body of Christ much more than in the past, and that the better known gifts of inspired speech will be expressed in greater beauty and edification in the Church.

It is our opinion that God wants the gifts to be active in the Christian's life to increase our own edification and joy, and also to make it clear to the world that Jesus is alive and real. The Holy Spirit divides the gifts to every man severally as He wills, and the Holy Spirit wills that we live an abundant life in Christ.

"Now unto Him that is able to do exceeding abundantly above all that we ask or think, according to the power that worketh in us, unto Him be glory in the Church by Christ Jesus throughout all ages, world without end" (Eph. 3:20 KJV).

14
The Excellent Way

In Exodus 28 we read a description of the vestments of the high priest, worn when he served in the tabernacle in worship of God. The high priest had a garment called an *ephod*. It was blue, and around the hem had a very special decoration:

"And beneath upon the hem of it thou shalt make pomegranates of blue, and of purple, and of scarlet, round about the hem thereof; and bells of gold between them round about: a golden bell and a pomegranate, a golden bell and a pomegranate, upon the hem of the robe round about" (Exod. 28:33 KJV).

The golden bells may be taken to symbolize the gifts of the Holy Spirit. The gifts are seen and heard, and they are beautiful. The bells sounded as the high priest moved in the Holy Place, invisible to the worshipers outside, but they knew he was praying for them. So the gifts show us that Jesus, although invisible to our earthly eyes, is alive and ministering for us in the Holy Place.

The pomegranates represent the fruit of the Spirit. They are sweet in flavor and attractive in color, and are loaded with seeds, and thus not only remind us of fruit, but of *fruitfulness*. We have made quite an extensive study of the gifts of the Holy Spirit, the golden bells, and now we must be careful to remind you that the gifts of the Spirit are balanced by the fruit of the Spirit.

The gifts of the Spirit (I Cor. 12:7–11 KJV), again, are: wisdom, knowledge, discerning of spirits, faith, miracles, healing, prophecy, tongues, and interpretation of tongues; the fruit of the Spirit (Gal. 5:22–23) is: love, joy, peace, patience, gentleness, kindness, faith, humility, and discipline. Believer-priests today should check the hem of their robes, that is, their lives, to see what is there.

In order for there to be a "golden bell and a pomegranate, a golden bell and a pomegranate" as the Scripture says, around the robe of the priest, there would have to be an equal number of each. It is interesting to see in the preceding lists that there are exactly nine gifts and nine fruit of the Spirit. In order for the golden bells to ring clearly, harmoniously, without clashing into one another, there must be fruit between each one.

Gifts brought through lives that are lacking in fruit, and motivated by a desire for self-esteem and a wish to be noticed, will be about as uplifting as so many clanging tin cans. The gifts of the Spirit are given "without repentance"—that is, God does not take them back because they are misused—and so they may function through lives that are unconsecrated, and through persons who need to make restitution to God and man; but these would be nothing more than ear-shattering brass bells to those who have discernment. This is what the Apostle means when he speaks of "sounding brass" and "clanging cymbals." Our bells should not be brass or tin, but pure gold. Golden bells represent lives that are in tune with the Lord and the brethren, and whose central desire is to lift up Jesus Christ, as they manifest the gifts.

It's significant that this pattern of the alternate bells and pomegranates carries into the New Testament, since between the two great chapters on the gifts, I Corinthians 12 and 14, is found the beautiful chapter on the central fruit of the Spirit—love—in I Corinthians 13:

"If I have the gift of being able to speak in languages
of men and of angels, without having learned them, but
have not love,
  I am like noisy brass bells,
  Or clanging cymbals.
And though I have been used in the gift of prophecy,
and understand all mysteries, and all knowledge;
And though I have the fullest measure of faith,
so that I could remove mountains,
    And have not love,
    I am nothing.
Though I give away all I have to the poor, and
give my body to be burned, and have not God's
love shining through me,
    It profits me nothing.
  Love is patient and kind;
  Love is not envious;
Love is not puffed up with pride,
Does not behave itself unmannerly or out of order,
  Seeks not her own way,
  Is not easily irritated,
  Entertains no evil thoughts;
Rejoices not at injustice and unrighteousness,
but rejoices when right and truth win;
    Love is consistent,
Love is always ready to trust,
Expects the best, in everything
    Endures as a good soldier.
    Love never ends;
As for prophecies, they will pass away; as for tongues,
they will cease; as for knowledge, it too will one day
    pass away.
For our knowledge is fragmentary and our prophecy is limited.

But when the Perfect comes, the imperfect will no longer be
   needed.
When I was a child, I spoke as a child, I reasoned as a child;
but when I became a man, I gave up childish ways.
For now we are looking in a mirror which gives a dim reflection,
but then we will see face to face!
   Now I understand in part,
but then will know fully, even as I have been known.
   So faith, hope, and love abide,
      these three;
but the greatest of these is love."

Love is the most important fruit of the Spirit; without it the
other eight fruit could not exist. They are called "fruit" instead
of "fruits" because the others are like sections of an orange con-
tained within the fruit of love.

What kind of love is this which is described as being greater
than faith, which is the key to the Bible, and without which we
can receive nothing from God? This love is spoken of as being
greater than knowledge, which is a gift of the Spirit, and one
greatly desired by Christians. It is greater than martyrdom for
our trust in Jesus! It is greater than giving to the poor, though
this is certainly a good thing to do. This love is greater than the
gift of prophecy, which Paul said all Christians should desire as
it is the greatest gift with which to edify the Church. It is greater
than speaking in unknown languages. It is greater than hope.

This must be speaking of a different kind of love from ordinary
human love, which is inconsistent and limited. In English we
have only one word for "love," whereas the Greek language has
seven! Only two of these are used in the New Testament, however: *philia*, which means affection or fondness for another as in
friendship—a limited kind of love; and *agape*, which means
God's perfect love—unconditional love—as expressed in the love

of God for man, or Christian brotherly love in its highest manifestation coming as a result of God living in man.

A third word for love in the Greek tongue is the familiar *eros*, which means physical or sensual love. Thus we have a trinity of words for "love": *agape*—spirit; *philia*—soul; *eros*—body.

The fruit of the Spirit we are talking about in this chapter is *agape*. God's love for man was shown to us through the birth, life, and death of Jesus Christ. "Greater love has no man than this, that a man lay down his life for his friends" (John 15:13 RSV)—and even His enemies (Rom. 5:7–10). God's love in man comes as a result of salvation. The baptism with the Holy Spirit causes a greater outflow of God's love, as long as the person is abiding in Christ and walking in the Spirit. "The love of God is shed abroad in our hearts by the Holy Ghost which is given unto us" (Rom. 5:5 KJV). First Corinthians 13 is speaking of *agape*, self-sacrificial love, love without reservation.

Love is not only the central fruit of the Spirit but a commandment from Jesus:

"Thou shalt love the Lord thy God with all thy heart, and with all thy soul, and with all thy mind. This is the first and great commandment. And the second is like unto it, Thou shalt love thy neighbour as thyself. On these two commandments hang all the law and the prophets" (Matt. 22:37–39 KJV).

Jesus also said: "A new commandment I give unto you, That you love one another; as I have loved you . . ." (John 13:34).

Love is also given in the New Testament as one of the things that "edifies" us spiritually. "Knowledge puffs up, but love edifies."

The beginning stage of love is when we can only love the one who loved us first. "We love him (God) because he first loved us" (I John 4:19 KJV). It is a necessary beginning, but a mixed love. With pure love comes a forgetting of self and a greater desire to give than to receive. As we do this we find ourselves loving God not for what He has done or is doing for us but loving Him for Himself alone.

Only after we have made connections with that heavenly resource of love, can we be expected to love our neighbors. The first and great commandment, to love God, had to come before the second, to love our neighbor, because without tapping into God's love it is impossible for us to love our fellowman.

God wouldn't have made this requirement if it were impossible for us. Some people say that loving God takes up all their time so that they have none left over to give to anyone else! Jesus commanded His disciples to love one another in the same manner as He had loved them, as a sign to the world that they were His followers. When we love the brethren we are loving Christ because the Bible says we are all the body of Christ, flesh of His flesh and bone of His bones (Eph. 5:29–30; I Cor. 12:27). God receives love from us *as we love* the brethren in Christ, as well as in our devotion to Him in prayer and praise. As we mature in love we will also be able to reach out and love the unbeliever, and even love and forgive our enemies (Matt. 5:43–48).

Love on an earthly plane, however, is impossible without loving yourself first, as the Scripture says: "Love your neighbor *as yourself.*" If you hate yourself you will not be able to truly love God, the brethren, the unbeliever, or your enemy. Only through knowing who you are in Christ, and that the essential you is a new creature where God dwells, can you ever love yourself. Only through Jesus is there anything worth loving in ourselves. It is a sin *not* to love ourselves. How can we help but love all that God has created?

Paul says at the end of the twelfth chapter: "Covet earnestly the best gifts: and yet I show unto you a more excellent way" (I Cor. 12:31). The more excellent way is not "instead of the gifts" but instead of "coveting the gifts": loving so much that the gifts flow forth in such beauty that they are as a refreshing river blessing all in their pathway.

Agape never fails, says Paul; but prophecy, tongues, knowledge, and the other gifts will vanish away when Jesus the Perfect One returns for His Church. The gifts are mainly for the edification and protection of the Church on earth, but when the Church is with the Edifier, the gifts will no longer be needed. But they are needed today.

A young man enlists in the army. We expect that he will develop "fruit" in his life—courage, stamina, perseverance, reliability, etc. The fruit are most important and are being established permanently in his character. What if this young man was sent to a war zone and told: "Now, son, you have the most important things; the fruit have really been developed in your life, and you don't need anything else." He would probably reply:

"Sir, that sounds very good, but I've heard rumors that there's an enemy around here, and the casualties coming in confirm the rumors. If you don't mind I'd like some weapons (gifts) to protect myself with; there's a war on!" If he were then told that the weapons had passed away because they were no longer needed by the army, he would be hard to convince!

Yes, there is a war on; and as long as we live in this fallen world, we will need the gifts. The gifts have not passed away yet; in fact Scripture indicates that before Jesus returns for His Church there will be an even greater moving of the Holy Spirit to combat the increased work of the enemy, and the gifts will obviously be included (Joel 2:23-24, 28-31; Hag. 2:9). One glorious day when the battle is over and won, the gifts will no longer be needed.

Faith and hope as we know it in this life shall also pass away. "Hope that is seen is not hope . . . but if we hope for that we see not, then do we with patience wait for it" (Rom. 8:24-25 KJV). "Now faith is the substance of things hoped for, the evidence of things not seen" (Heb. 11:1 KJV). Seeing the evidence of our faith will bring us into a different kind of faith relationship from what we have now. When we see Our Lord face to face, all these things shall pass away as the Scripture tells us. That which remains for Eternity will be love—*agape*—for "God is Love."

We have tried to show that there needs to be a balance and an interplay between the gifts and fruit of the Holy Spirit. The gifts, the golden bells, need to be ringing, to proclaim to the world that our great high priest is alive forevermore, and still doing His saving, healing work on earth through the ministry of His people. The fruit needs to be seen, in order to show people what Jesus is like and that He loves them. The world must see the love of God active in His people.

15
Consecration

We have talked about two basic Christian experiences: the most important being salvation and next, the baptism with the Holy Spirit. These are given freely to anyone who asks, and nothing can be done to earn them.

There is also a vital step we may call *consecration*.[1] The first two steps God offers to us for our simple acceptance, whereas in consecration we give ourselves back to God:

"I beseech you therefore, brethren . . . that you present your bodies a living sacrifice, holy [consecrated], acceptable unto God which is your reasonable service" (Rom. 12:1).

Paul is here speaking to the "brethren"—to believers who are saved and no doubt baptized in the Holy Spirit. Consecration is something that *we* do, but we can only do it because God gives us the ability. It is yielding our self-will to God to the fullest possible measure, so that His perfect will may be done in and through us. This step is a response to the prayer:

"Thy kingdom come, Thy will be done *in* earth [in earthen vessels (II Cor. 4:7)], as it is in heaven . . ." (Matt. 6:10 KJV).

It means really allowing Jesus to be King and Lord of our lives.

"Who . . . is willing to consecrate his service this day unto

[1] Other terms often used are: commitment, discipleship, or dedication.

the Lord?" King David asked the people (I Chron. 29:5 KJV). The children of Israel responded willingly and with a "perfect heart"; they gave of themselves and their substance for the building of the Temple of the Lord. Then David prayed a beautiful prayer ending with the familiar words:

"All things come of thee, and of thine own have we given thee" (I Chron. 29:14 KJV).

We, and all we have, belong to God, but having given us free will, He must wait for us to give all back to Him willingly.

Just as we are saved when we first receive Jesus, and yet our salvation continues, day by day; just as we receive the Holy Spirit, once and for all at a particular time, and yet must allow Him to fill us day by day; so we need to make an initial act of consecration which must be renewed also day by day, as we gather up the parts of our lives that seem to have gotten away from Him, and bring them back where they belong. There are many who have been born again and baptized in the Holy Spirit who don't realize the need for consecration. Yet consecration is the only way to a full and victorious Christian life.

Consecration then, is *choosing* to walk with Jesus every day; it means putting Jesus first in your life and going His way. "Seek first the kingdom of God, and His righteousness; and all these things shall be added unto you" (Matt. 6:33). Jesus promises always to be with you, but the unconsecrated believer makes Jesus accompany him where he wants to go, while the consecrated person follows Jesus where *He* wants to go. Jesus said: "If any man will come after me, let him deny himself, and take up his cross daily [yield his self-will daily] and follow me" (Luke 9:23 KJV).

Some may say at this point: "This all sounds very good but how can I learn to do it?" One of the best helps found is the discovery of the difference between soul and spirit. We've mentioned before the importance of seeing that we are not two parts, soul and body, like the animals; but three parts: Spirit, soul, and body.

The spirit (*pneuma*) is the innermost part of us which was created to have fellowship with God. It was dead in "trespasses and sins," and came alive when we became Christians, and God came to live there. Within our spirit is that place of an inner knowing or witness to the will of God. The Book of Colossians says: "For in him [Jesus] dwelleth all the fulness of the Godhead [Trinity] bodily. And you [the Christian] are complete in him" (Col. 2:9–10). In the Gospel of John, Jesus says: "If a man love me, he will keep my words: and my Father will love him, and we will come unto him, and make our abode with him" (John 14:23 KJV), and "I will pray the Father, and he shall give you another Comforter, that he may abide with you for ever" (John 14:16 KJV). With the Father, Son, and Holy Spirit living in our spirit, what more can we ask for? This is the part of us called the "new creature" where our spirit and the Holy Spirit have been joined together and have become one (I Cor. 6:17). This is too often the most neglected part of our being; yet it is the most important.

The soul (*psyche*) is the part of man that has ruled him ever since the fall. It has three parts: intellect, will, and emotions. The soul in the Christian is in the state of being straightened out; it is still a mixture of good and evil. When the soul is yielded to God it is wonderful—when it is not, it can seriously block what God wants to do in and through us. Although the "old man" was crucified with Christ, the mess he left from the time he was in charge is still in our soul; the cleanup job in scriptural language is called sanctification. This area is a real battleground! It is the area of the "self" which Jesus calls us to deny.

The body (*soma*) is the area of the five senses: tasting, touching, smelling, seeing, and hearing. The body is the house of the soul and the spirit, and the Christian's body becomes the temple of the *Holy* Spirit (I Cor. 6:19). With the baptism in the Holy Spirit it is filled to overflowing with the glory of God. As long as our bodies—which still have fallen tendencies—do not control our lives, but rather are controlled by the Holy Spirit and our "new creature" life, they will express the beauty and joy of the Lord. God has a plan for our physical bodies, and will bring it to pass as we are obedient to the promptings of the Holy Spirit and His Word concerning His temple. God wants you to "prosper and be in health even as your soul prospers" (III John 1:2).

Our situation in life might be compared to a great ocean liner. The captain has been critically ill, and unable to command the ship for a long time. The crew know very well how to work the ship, and so they have taken over. Unfortunately, they really do not know where they are going, or what the voyage is all about, so they have been sailing aimlessly over the ocean. They have been quarreling among themselves, and the ship is nearly out of fuel. Since they don't know how to navigate or how to get to port, they can't refuel. Things are in pretty bad shape! Miraculously, the captain recovers, but he finds it is going to take him a while to gain control of the ship again. Now and then the crew listen to him, but most of the time they say: "Now, sir, we have been sailing this vessel around for a long time without your help, and we know how to do it. Just let us alone!"

Your spirit in union with the Holy Spirit is supposed to be the ruler of your soul, and your submitted soul is supposed to direct your body. For a long time, however, ever since you were born, your spirit has been out of action, and your soul and body have been running things for themselves. How is the captain of the ship going to get his position back? What the crew doesn't know is there will be true happiness only when the captain with his charts and compass and knowledge of the sea is allowed to take complete command. The captain also knows how the radio works and can call for help and instructions, for fuel, and other needed supplies. Only with the captain in charge will peace and joy reign on the ship!

For the Christian, right after his baptism in the Holy Spirit, God's Presence is so real that it is no effort to put God first. He's first on his mind in the morning, the favorite topic of conversation through the day, and last on his mind before retiring at night. His renewed spirit (the captain) is on top and his soul (the crew) and the body (the ship) are functioning according to the captain's directions. In some, this peace and order lasts longer than in others, but soon the soul begins to contend for its former place of control. To keep things in the right order the Christian needs to understand the difference between his *soul* and his *spirit*. He can know this through study and application of the Scriptures.

"The word of God is quick, and powerful, and sharper than any two-edged sword, piercing even to the dividing asunder of soul and spirit, and of the joints and marrow, and is a discerner of the thoughts and intents of the heart" (Heb. 4:12 KJV).

Why does the Scripture tell us of the need to divide or separate between the soul and spirit? The soul, as we've said, is still a mixture of good and evil. The Bible never tells us to walk in the soul or live in the soul, but it does say over and over again, "walk in the spirit," "live in the spirit," "pray in the spirit," "sing in the spirit"! Only as we learn to walk in the spirit, with our souls in a place of submission to God's Spirit, can our souls be cleansed, healed, restored, and used to His glory. The Psalmist David's words are appropriate here:

"He leads me beside still waters; he restores my soul" (Ps. 23:2–3 RSV).

Just as we are three parts: spirit, soul, and body, our souls also have three parts: intellect, will, and emotions. Our *intellect* is one of the most difficult areas of our soul to yield to the work of the Holy Spirit. It seems to have fallen the farthest in original sin, as it was through the reaching out of the intellect into areas forbidden by God that sin entered the world. The tempter said:

"For God knows that in the day you eat there of, then your eyes will be opened, and you will be as gods, knowing good and evil" (Gen. 3:5).

Man has lived by the reasonings of his fallen intellect ever since. We're taught from the first grade that the intellect is the greatest part of our lives, but education isn't the complete answer to change our world. (Dennis' mother used to say: "If you educate a devil, you just get a clever devil!") Satan is slicker than the world's greatest criminal lawyer; he certainly will fool our intellect if that's strictly what we're going by. Our mind has accumulated good and bad, true and false information, and even after conversion and the baptism with the Holy Spirit, it takes time to be changed. The intellect is wonderful, though, when submitted to God and renewed by the Holy Spirit.

"And be not conformed to this world: but be transformed [transformed and transfigured come from the same Greek word *metamorphöo*—where we get the word metamorphosis] by the renewing of your mind, that you may prove what is the . . . perfect, will of God" (Rom. 12:2). The Scripture also says:

"Let this mind be in you, which was also in Christ Jesus" (Phil. 2:5 KJV).

Don't accept every thought that pops into your mind as yours. Check to be sure of its origin by asking yourself: Did this come from God? Did this come from my new life in Christ? Or did this come from the enemy? The enemy's fiery darts and evil imaginations need to be cast out of your life immediately. Temptation is not sin, but entertaining temptation is, and it will eventually lead to wrong actions. The Bible says:

"Casting down imaginations, and every high thing that exalteth itself against the knowledge of God, and bringing into captivity every thought to the obedience of Christ" (II Cor. 10:5 KJV).

The "knowledge of God" is that the believer is a new creature, and so his thoughts will be healthy and good. All other thoughts come from the enemy or from the soul life and should be resisted. The believer must continuously oppose these wrong thoughts (it will get easier as he goes along), or he may return to many of his old ways. Watchman Nee,[2] the great Chinese spiritual leader, says that there are many of God's children who have new hearts but old heads.

The words "casting down" in the preceding passage indicate that our cooperation is needed, and here's where our will comes in. The *will* is the central part of the soul, where choices and decisions are made. It is the essential self, and has been used for self-will instead of God's will. God gave man a free will so that he could freely choose to love Him, but man's wrong use of free will, to reject God, cost the death of Jesus. Free will was purchased by Jesus' death. God never takes free will away from us, but each day we show Him our love by freely giving our will back to Him. This is what consecration is all about.

God is not interested in having us "automatically" obey Him because we have no will of our own. This would be a travesty of scriptural teaching. It is what the so-called perennial philosophy, the intellectual mysticism which man concocts, comes up with, but it is entirely foreign to the Judaeo-Christian way of thinking. Those who accept God's revealing of Himself in the Scripture, and especially in Jesus Christ, know that God wants creatures who willingly want what He desires for them. They do not lose their wills; they consciously, actively, and with joy, bring their wills into conformity with His, because they feel and know His love, and because they are responding to His love. God gave us free will, the power to choose, so that we could freely love and freely obey Him. God wants children, not robots. The Father longs for His children's obedience, because He loves them

[2] We recommend many of Watchman Nee's books to you: *Sit, Walk, Stand, Release of the Spirit,* and *Changed Into His Likeness* to name a few.

and wants to bring them to the very best. The children desire to obey the Father, because they love Him.

Jesus, whose will was sinless and thus different from ours, set an example for us. He said:

"I seek not my own will, but the will of the Father who sent me" (John 5:30).

You may have been afraid to yield your will to God because the enemy has scared you by saying such things as: "God will surely make you leave your family and will send you to some far-off country," or "God will make you stand on a street corner in your hometown and preach to the passersby!" Don't listen to him!

Settle in your mind once and for all that God loves you and wants only the best for you; only in going according to His plan will you bear the most fruitful life now and through eternity! We must let nothing hold us back from God's best!

The will also controls that third part of our soul: our *emotions*. Emotions are the "feelings" of the soul. Some Christians have emotions much like a Yo-Yo! Today they feel "saved"; tomorrow they feel "unsaved." Today they feel God is really guiding them; tomorrow they're not sure if He knows they exist. The novelist George Macdonald describes it thus:

"They had a feeling, or a feeling had them, till another feeling came and took its place. When a feeling was there, they felt as if it would never go; when it was gone they felt as if it had never been; when it returned, they felt as if it had never gone." [3]

Obviously our emotions are undependable, and if we try to guide our lives by them it will lead to confusion. In the past we have misused our emotions: letting our temper fly, giving way to self-pity, etc. Our lives can't be directed by our feelings; they too are a mixture of good and evil. We must go by that inner knowing in our spirits which is in agreement with God's Word. "Feel-

[3] George Macdonald, *What's Mine's Mine* (New York: McKay, 1886), chap. 16.

ings aren't facts." This doesn't mean that a Christian's life should be devoid of emotion, but that God has a work of healing and renewing in this part of our lives to perform also.

The step of consecration—greatly assisted by learning to divide between soul and spirit—needs to be taken if it's not yet a reality in our lives. It's something we must consent to, and when we do, it deepens and establishes the rest in our souls. It is no accident that the fourth chapter of Hebrews speaks of entering God's rest just before telling of the need to divide or distinguish between soul and spirit. Choosing to live in the spirit instead of in the soul brings this rest, but many Christians have yet to learn the difference. Salvation is a rest in the spirit of man: "Repent therefore, and be converted, that your sins may be blotted out, when the times of refreshing shall come from the presence of the Lord" (Acts 3:19). Jesus said: "Come to Me, all you that labour and are heavy laden, and I will give you rest" (Matt. 11:28). The baptism with the Holy Spirit is an outflowing of that rest bringing a rest in the soul. Isaiah puts it this way: "For with stammering lips and another tongue will he speak to this people. To whom he said, This is the rest wherewith you may cause the weary to rest; and this is the refreshing . . ." (Isa. 28:11–12). The intellect comes into rest as it is yielded to God, and praying in tongues is one important means of letting the Holy Spirit renew and refresh our minds and souls. As we learn to deny our souls the right to rule us and walk in that rest with our souls and spirits submitted to the Lord, then God can get rid of the "wood, hay, and stubble" and establish those things of permanent value in our lives (I Cor. 3:12–13). Jesus said:

"Take my yoke upon you, and learn of me; for I am meek and lowly in heart: and you shall find rest unto your souls" (Matt. 11:29).

"Take My yoke upon you." Even as one ox (you) is led by the other (Jesus), the two being yoked together—both are servants and burden bearers—the one in the lead guides the other in the way, and bears the heaviest load. When we begin to feel the weight of the load, we can be sure that we're taking the lead away from Our Lord and need to get back into our place—one step behind Him. The heaviness of the load is like a spiritual thermometer to warn us that the soul is taking the lead and not the Spirit. The heaviness reveals that our souls are not resting in Christ.

Let's be careful not to revert back to functioning out of the fallen intellect, emotions, and self-will, but instead continue that flow which began at our Pentecost: the mind of Christ manifesting in us, His emotions flowing through us, and His will being done by us.

Here is a prayer you might like to use, or you may want to pray using your own words:

Dear Heavenly Father,

Thank you so much for the wonderful gifts of salvation and the baptism in the Holy Spirit. Words are inadequate to express my gratitude! I know these gifts were free, given to me, on no merit of my own, but just because You love me. Now I want to give You the only thing I have to give . . . myself. I know Your will for my life is marvelous and so I ask that Your perfect will be done in and through me, from this day on. Help my will to yield to Yours until they blend together as one. I ask Your Son, Jesus Christ, to come and take the throne of my life and reign as Lord.

I know I can't do this in my own strength, but I'm relying on Your daily guidance and strength to help me. Thank You, Father, for hearing my prayer. Praise Your Name!

In Jesus' Name I pray,
Amen

16
The Narrow Way

Jesus said: "Narrow is the way which leadeth unto life" (Matt. 7:14 KJV). He didn't say: "Hard is the way," He said it was *narrow*. On the other hand He also said: "My yoke is easy, and my burden is light" (Matt. 11:30 KJV); and "Fear not, little flock; for it is your Father's good pleasure to *give* you the kingdom!" (Luke 12:32 KJV). Nothing could be more delightful than walking the King's Highway. One of the great Christians of the Middle Ages said: "God gives us a little bit of heaven to go to heaven in!" The road to heaven is glorious—illuminated by the love of God, and the fellowship of friends in Jesus. The Scripture says: "If we walk in the light, as he is in the light, we have fellowship one with another, and the blood of Jesus Christ cleanseth us from all sin" (I John 1:7 KJV). The Christian Way isn't difficult in itself, it is made difficult by the attacks of the enemy, who wants to push us off the track. Jesus said: "In the world you will have trouble, but be of good cheer, I have conquered the world!" (John 16:33). The difficult things don't come from God, but from the challenges of the world, the flesh, and the devil. If we stay on the "narrow way" and are not frightened by the attacks, if we don't listen to the lies of the enemy, we will have no difficulty in applying Jesus' victory to the situation, and

187

walking on in triumph and joy, no matter what happens. God doesn't want us defeated, but victorious.

When Jesus speaks of the "narrow way," He means that the true path is a very thin line between extremes. Think of it in terms of navigation. When a big airliner is flying across the Pacific to the Hawaiian Islands, it is flying a narrow way. There is a certain compass heading which, according to the charts, will take that aircraft to the destination, but if the captain were to take up that heading—say of 225°—and simply hold to it all the way across the water, he would most certainly miss his destination. His instruments aren't that accurate, for one thing, and for another, winds and turbulent air would combine to throw him off course. What actually happens is that the navigator is busy correcting the course all the way along, and instead of flying by "dead reckoning," the course is being checked all the time by other means. It takes effort to stay on that "narrow way," that tiny thin line across the trackless waters that leads to the Honolulu airport! This is the sort of thing Jesus is talking about when He speaks of the "narrow way"—it is that one correct road, that one correct heading that leads to heaven. In order to stay on that heading, we have to be continually correcting our course by the chart, that is, by the Word of God, and by the sightings we take, that is, by our experience of God.

Satan has many devices to delay us if he can. Most people are on the alert for the obvious ones. They can see the danger in out-and-out temptations—violations of the moral law: murder, theft, adultery, etc. But the more subtle ones are the dangerous ones. If someone wanted to stop you from getting on a horse and riding, say, to a town ten miles away, there are several ways he might accomplish his purpose. First of all, he might try to persuade you that horses are not safe. "I once had an uncle who was kicked by a horse, and spent three weeks in the hospital!" he might say. So Satan tries to persuade people that religion in general is dangerous. "Leave it alone—you'll go off the deep end!" he'll say. "Why, look at so-and-so! You don't want to get like him, do you?"

If he fails in this, and sees that you are going to get "on the horse" anyway, then he changes his tune completely: "I'll help you!" he says, and tries to give you such a boost into the saddle, that you fall off the other side and bump your head! In other words, he sees that you are going to try God, so he arranges for you to encounter some peculiar things at the very beginning that will frighten you. He tries to get you to a meeting where people are not observing decency and order, or where there are obvious false teachings, and "strange" people, so as to cause you to "bump your head" right from the start. Some people are backed off for years by one bad experience, when they thought they would like to find out about God, and encountered some "way-out" people.[1]

If, however, you get firmly seated in the saddle, his next gambit is to send you in the wrong direction! Especially when people are new in their journey on the "narrow way," the enemy tries to get them involved in "new gospels," [2] and strange doctrines. He loves to say: "Look at the people in your church, in your prayer group—they are just 'milk and water Christians'! They're just 'babes in Christ.' You'd better go and join Brother X's organization. They are teaching some new doctrines. The Lord's

[1] We quite often meet folk who, when confronted by the "charismatic renewal" will say:

"Oh, forty years ago I went to a 'Holy Roller' meeting across the tracks in the little town where I was brought up. They were really carrying on. I don't want anything to do with *that!*" This is just as if a person might say:

"Oh, I had a ride in a 1917 Model T Ford back in 1923. It was awful. We broke down five times in twenty miles. It was dusty, and bumpy. I certainly don't want anything to do with automobiles, if they're like that! I'll walk, thank you!" On the other hand, if the same people encounter "Model T" practices today, one cannot blame them if they get discouraged!

[2] Paul says: "Though we, or an angel from heaven, preach any other gospel unto you than that which we have preached unto you, let him be accursed" (Gal. 1:8).

given them a special word. They're special people. They're going to get to heaven first, and get a higher seat than anyone!"

If he can't get you involved with strange doctrines, if he can't get you to "come out" and join some separated brethren, then he'll send you some "Judaizers"—that is, some folk who are like the Jewish Christians who troubled the Gentile converts: "We're glad that you have met Jesus Christ, and received the Holy Spirit. You realize, however, that Jesus was the Messiah of the *Jews,* and you Gentiles must now keep the Jewish laws!" So these good souls say:

"Now, we're real happy that you got into the kingdom so easily, but now that you're in, you've got to start keeping the law, just like the rest of us! You haven't been properly baptized, for a start! Then you must change your manner of dress; take off your lipstick—or your loud neckties, let your hair grow—or, if you are a man, cut your hair—and be like us!"

Or the "dispensationalists" may make a "pass" at you: "We're real glad you have had this wonderful experience which *you* call the baptism in the Holy Spirit," they may say. "What really happened was that you finally got *saved!* Speaking in tongues, and all those things are not for today. We'll come and give you Bible lessons and explain it all away for you!"

But if you insist on riding the right way, then Satan's last attempt will be to stampede you! He says: "Good! You're going in the right direction. Now you'd better not waste any time! Hurry up!" And so he tries to get you to go overboard. "Speaking in tongues? By all means!" says he. "As often as possible! Interrupt the preacher at your church on Sunday morning. He doesn't believe in speaking in tongues—so you *show* him! Witness? By all means! Tell everybody! Bend everyone's ear at all times! Don't ever talk about anything else! Buttonhole all your friends! Ask them if they're saved, and the more you embarrass them the better! It'll show how fearless you are!" If you repel this attack, he'll just trot along beside you on the journey and renew his various attempts. But if you resist him and pay no attention to his lies, he has no further power over you. Satan's power lies mainly in his lying tongue. It is through this that he gains power, first over your mind, and then over your body. Shut him out!

The "narrow way" is, then, a true course between extremes. In II Timothy 2:15 we read: "Study to show yourself approved unto God, a workman that needs not to be ashamed, rightly dividing the word of truth." The original Greek on this reads:

"Be diligent to present yourself approved unto God, a workman not ashamed, cutting the word of truth correctly." The word "correctly cutting"—*orthotomeo*—does not mean to cut the truth up into sections or pieces, as some dispensational teachers have used it, but it means to cut a straight or correct path to a goal. It would be used of pioneers cutting a track through a forest, or across an unexplored wilderness, and thus agrees exactly with the idea of the "narrow way."

The narrow way is not a compromise, as some will try to tell you. Being in balance between extremes doesn't limit how far you can go. A railroad train stays on the "narrow way"—on the track, that is—and it can go for thousands of miles, and at very high speeds. If it got off the track, it would soon stop, and very drastically! A building that is kept in balance over its foundations can be built as high as you like! So there is no limit to how far you can go and still remain at the right distance from the extremes.

What are some of the extremes through which we are called to cut a balanced path? Well, to begin with, there is the balance between freedom and legalism. Jesus expressed the "narrow way" perfectly Himself when he warned His followers to "beware of the leaven of the Pharisees, and of the leaven of Herod." The Pharisees were the legalists, who insisted that a man would be saved by keeping every detail of the law. Herod, on the other hand, stood for compromise and "anything goes"—libertinism.

So today there are those who want to be completely free of all restraint. "We are the children of God," say they. "All things are ours! We can do as we please!" On the other hand, there are the legalists who would like to take all freedom away from the Christian, and put him under interminable "thou shalts," and "thou shalt nots." The middle way here was well expressed by St. Augustine, in his memorable saying: "*Habe caritatem, et fac quod vis.*" "Have the love of God in you (*agape*), and do what you will!" When you are guided by God's love you will want to do what pleases Him.

There is the narrow way between those who emphasize the need for Christians to share Christ's suffering and death, and those who emphasize His Risen Life. St. Paul holds these in balance beautifully when he says: "That I may know him, and the power of his resurrection, and the fellowship of his sufferings, being made conformable unto his death; If by any means I might attain unto the resurrection of the dead" (Phil. 3:10–11 KJV).

The narrow way cuts between those who say that a Christian should possess nothing, and those who seem to feel that he should be a millionaire! Here again it is the Apostle Paul who points out the "narrow way": "I know both how to be abased, and I know how to abound: every where and in all things I am instructed both to be full and to be hungry, both to abound and to suffer need. I can do all things through Christ who strengthens me" (Phil. 4:12–13).

The way goes between those who want to emphasize the humanity of Jesus, and those who want to see only His divinity. The true path shows us God Who is Man, and Man Who is God.

It cuts between those who would present the Christian life as a matter of individual salvation only—concerned only with the individual's relationship with God—and those who focus entirely on the "group," as though God dealt with people only in "bunches"!

It cuts between those who emphasize *religious experience* and those who emphasize *objective truth*. The *Spirit* and the *Word* must go together, and of that we want to talk in detail in the next chapter.

17
The Charts

To travel any distance you need a chart—a map that clearly shows you where you are going, and what lies along the way. The believer's "chart" is the Holy Scriptures. The Anglican *Book of Common Prayer* says, speaking of the Scriptures, that we are to "read, learn, mark, and inwardly digest" them[1]—one of the most important pieces of advice for a believer who wants to move steadily along the King's Highway.

Read the Scriptures. Let the Bible be your main Book. Some great men and women of God have read little else! Equip yourself with several different versions and translations. If you read, even with difficulty, another language, be sure to get a copy of the Bible in that language. Every version or translation reflects the attitude of the reviser or translator, but if you compare several, you begin to get a picture "in depth" of the real meaning of a passage. Of course, the ideal would be to be able to read the original in Hebrew and Greek. You may not have the time to learn these languages, but if you are serious about your New Testament study you should get an *Interlinear Greek-English New Testament*, which has the literal translation of the Greek words immediately under them. Even if you know no Greek at

---

[1] *Book of Common Prayer*, p. 92.

all, you will find this book interesting and informative; with a very little effort you can learn the Greek letters; and with the help of a Greek-English lexicon, a Greek concordance, and a minimum of grammar, you can learn a lot. If this sounds formidable, how much effort and expense would you put into learning, say, to play golf, or to ski? Should you not be prepared to spend at least that much on learning God's Word?

Don't read little "snatches" of Scripture! Read it in big chunks —at least several chapters a day. How much time do you spend reading the newspaper? Watching TV? Reading the latest magazine? Reading the latest best seller? How does your time reading the Bible compare?

It isn't a good idea to begin at the beginning of the Bible and read straight through to the end, as if it were a novel! The name of the Holy Scriptures in Greek is *Ta Biblia,* which means *The Books.* The Bible is a symposium of writings, different, and yet all on the same theme, because they were all inspired by the same Holy Spirit. Each book in the Bible supports and enhances the others, and yet each one is a unit in itself. Some books, of course, are like a serial story—I and II Kings, I and II Chronicles, Luke and Acts, the first five books (the Pentateuch), etc. Some of the most difficult parts of the Bible to understand are the very first books; so if you are reading the Bible seriously for the first time, you should begin with the Gospels, which tell of the life, death, and rising again of the Lord Jesus Christ. Then go on to the Acts of the Apostles, which tells of the doings of some of the earliest Christians. As you read the Acts, you can read the letters of Paul (Epistles) that he wrote to the places he visited. You will want to explore the Epistles written by others besides Paul. Now you can start at Genesis and read of the beginnings, then follow with the story of the patriarchs and the rise and fall of God's people of the Old Testament. Here you can read the books of the Prophets and the histories of Job, Esther, and Ruth. You will find that Psalms and Proverbs make excellent daily reading. Finally, you may want to dip into the very difficult Book of Revelation, which tells of the "last things."

As a Christian baptized in the Holy Spirit, you will find the Bible speaking to you all the way through, even though you do not always understand the background of what you are reading. This is the most important use of the Scriptures, to let the Holy Spirit speak to you, and of this we'll have more to say a little later.

There are lots of books available that will help you to set up a plan of Bible-reading and study. You will need some commentaries, that is, books written to help you understand, verse by verse, what the Bible is talking about. Be very careful in your selection of these commentaries—just as careful as you would be in picking a live teacher to help you. Avoid those that are the work of modernist scholars, many of whom do not believe in the divinity of Jesus, or in His saving work. Use the older commentaries, unless you are sure that the modern one you have is written by a person sound in the faith.

If possible, get into a good Bible class, with a believing teacher. We strongly recommend that you find a teacher who has received the baptism in the Holy Spirit. If you can't get a "live" teacher, records and tapes provide an excellent resource. They are a good supplement to class teaching, too. There are some good radio ministries. In all things you must be selective and discerning.

Watch out for "proof texts." It is not what a particular verse in the Bible teaches that we must focus on, but what the *whole* Bible teaches. Most false teachings are built on an isolated verse or verses of the Scripture, taken out of context, and blown up out of proportion. The better you know the whole Book, the better you will be able to deal with the person who uses isolated "proof texts." For example, those misled people who deny the threefold nature of God (the Trinity) quote Jesus saying: "I and My Father are One!" or, "He that hath seen Me, hath seen the Father!" in an attempt to prove that Jesus and the Father are one Person, but Christians don't believe in the threefold nature of God because of proof texts, but because the Trinity is presented in the Bible from start to finish—even though the word "Trinity" is not used. The Bible instead uses the word "Godhead" when speaking of the threefold God: Father, Son, and Holy Ghost. On the very first page of the Scriptures we read: "In the beginning, God created the heaven and earth . . . and the Spirit of God moved upon the face of the waters" (Gen. 1: 1–2 KJV). In the first chapter of the Gospel according to John we are told: "In the beginning was the Word, and the Word was with God, and the Word was God. The same was in the beginning with God. All things were made by him [the Word] and without him was not any thing made that was made. In Him was life; and the life was the light of men . . ." (John 1:1–4 KJV). And Who is the "Word"? We read on: "And the Word was made flesh, and dwelt among us, (and we beheld his glory, the glory as of the only begotten of the Father,) full of grace and truth" (John 1:14). So the Word which was in the very beginning with the Father, is none other than Jesus Christ—the "Word made flesh." Thus we see the Father, Son, and Holy Ghost at the creation. Are there other Scriptures to back up the fact that the Father created all things through Jesus Christ? Yes, for the Apostle Paul says it in so many words in Col. 1:16: "For by Him were all things created, that are in heaven, and that are on earth . . . all things were created by Him and for Him." Then in the first chapter of Hebrews we read: "God . . . has in these last days spoken unto us by His Son . . . by whom also He made the worlds" (Heb. 1:1-2). In the Gospels we are presented with the record of the baptism of Jesus, and are shown the Son of

God standing in Jordan, the Father speaking from heaven, and the Holy Ghost descending upon Jesus. Many times in the Gospels Jesus speaks of His Father in heaven, and He promises to send the Holy Spirit to take His, Jesus', place, after He has gone back to the Father. In Acts 7:55 we read: "But he (Stephen), being full of the Holy Ghost, looked up . . . and saw . . . Jesus standing on the right hand of God." Here again, the three Persons of the Trinity are clearly distinguished. In II Corinthians 13:14, Paul says: "The grace of the Lord Jesus Christ, and the love of God, and the communion of the Holy Ghost, be with you all . . ." Thus all the way through the Bible, we find reference after reference that keeps pointing us to the fact that God is Father, Son, and Holy Ghost—three distinct Persons in one Godhead. This should be our test with any doctrine—not what does one verse say, but what is the teaching of the *Scripture*.

Inspiration. Intellectual understanding and training in the faith is very important, but the most important ministry of the Bible to you will be *inspiration*. You need to let God speak to you personally through His Word. The Christian life must be an interplay of *experience* and *truth*. To return to our original illustration: if you set out to find the Hawaiian Islands without a chart, you may have many exciting experiences, but you won't get where you want to go! So if you simply set out, as many do, to have "spiritual experiences," you may have an exciting time, but you will be almost certain to end in confusion. Indeed, you will be in far greater danger than if you were navigating the ocean without a map, because there at least you are confronted only with the impersonal forces of wind and wave, but in the spiritual realm you are surrounded by enemies whose chief design is to lead you astray, and destroy you. However, if someone handed you a chart of the Pacific Ocean, pointed out the route to Hawaii and said: "There you are! You've got the chart; now you don't need to make the trip!" you would not be satisfied. The purpose of the chart is that you might see and enjoy the

Islands; it is not an end in itself. So the purpose of reading the Bible is that we might come to a deeper personal experience of God; then for every wonderful experience of God in our lives, there must come a scriptural understanding of what it means, which prepares us for further experience. The *Spirit* and the *Word* must be in continual interplay in order to keep the balance. In Heaven we will finally know the complete blending of the two, as God grants us full experience of Him, with full understanding.

Therefore, spend part of your time reading the Bible just waiting for the Holy Spirit to speak to you from its pages. When you do this, be prepared for some surprising insights, and some unexpected interpretations! The Holy Spirit can use the Scripture very freely and allegorically when He chooses. You may see a profound spiritual truth for your life in very unlikely places. A factual description of some aspect of the Temple, or an unlikely spot in a long list of names, may suddenly strike you with spiritual significance. When you try to share it with someone else, they may look at you blankly—but don't be disheartened by that. *That* little morsel was for you! The Rev. J. A. Dennis, of Austin, Texas, tells in his testimony how he was healed by laying hold of a promise for him from the Scripture! He was suffering from stomach trouble, and the Holy Spirit showed him the text: "I will take sickness away from the *midst* of thee!" (Exod. 23:25 KJV). "That's for me!" said J. A. Dennis. "In the midst of me, in my stomach, I've got trouble. God will take it away!" And God did take it away, and healed him completely! Later on, the Rev. Mr. Dennis told this to a well-trained Bible scholar, who laughed and said: "But *that* isn't what that verse means!" J. A. Dennis was healed, just the same, because the Holy Spirit said: "That's what *I* want it to mean to you, to build your faith!" This kind of inspiration is for blessing, not for doctrine.

When you begin to read the Bible, you will find many things you don't understand. Worse yet, you will find things you don't *like!* You will find things that seem contradictory. That's all right; it isn't because the Bible is defective, it's just because you don't yet comprehend. The answer to the seeming contradiction lies beyond your field of vision. Don't reject the thing you don't understand; just put it aside and say: "I don't get it, Lord! I don't even like it! But I'll just wait until You explain it to me. In the meantime I'll thank You for what I *do* understand!"

Mark your Bible! The *Book of Common Prayer* quotation we have been using didn't literally mean to "mark with a pencil or pen," but "pay strict attention to"; nevertheless, we can interpret it to mean: "Underline the words in your Bible that speak to you." Develop your own system of marking. You may want to get a loose-leaf Bible, or a pre-marked Bible, or a wide-margin Bible—check and see the different helps there are to *marking* your Bible.

Learn! Memorize the Scripture. Set out to learn whole passages and even whole books by heart. It's not as hard as you think, and it's a great way to emphasize what is there. Some married couples are memorizing by learning alternate verses—the husband takes one and the wife the next. This is good, because it is shared, and also when you learn this way, both really learn the whole passage. Remember that behind the Iron Curtain in many places Bibles are forbidden. There may come a time when you will wish you had learned more of the Scriptures by heart. The Scripture tells us of the Holy Spirit that He will "bring all things to our remembrance"—but He can't very well do that if you have never put them into your memory! It's true that the Holy Spirit can, if He chooses, give you a passage of Scripture that you have never heard before, but for the most part He works by quickening your memory. Don't be worried if you forget a passage after having once memorized it. You haven't really forgotten it. It's still there, down in your mind. It's just that you have lost track of it for the time being, but the Holy Ghost can fish it out when He wants to! Put it *in* there—that's the important thing! [1]

Inwardly digest! Let the Word of God become a part of you. Thus you make yourself more sensitive to God, and also more able to recognize that which is not of God. "That doesn't sound like God!" the person who knows his Bible will say, upon hearing false teaching. "That isn't the way God acts in the Bible!"

Carry a Bible with you at all times, but not a great big one; for that will frighten people! I Carry a little one, which will fit into your pocket or your purse. When you have some time during the day, you can read the Word. When you are witnessing, you can use your Bible. The Holy Scripture is the "Sword of the Spirit," so don't go about unarmed!

Theology. Don't be frightened by the word. Theology is simply the *summary* of what the *Bible* teaches about *God.* It might be termed the "truth about the truth about the Truth"! It is true that the Bible is the summary of our belief and practice, but it is also true that we need a summary of what is in the Bible! You can't very well read the whole Bible to everyone, or take the time to go through the entire Book and give all the references on every occasion. Theology is really such a summary, and the conclusions drawn from it. For example, we showed already how the Bible presents God all the way through as Father, Son, and Holy Ghost—as three Persons in one Godhead. Theology gives to this the title the "doctrine of the Trinity," and points out how it answers some difficult questions. To illustrate, if there were only one Person in the Godhead—if the Father,

---

[1] We have found a simple 3 x 5 file card a useful aid to memorizing. Take a fairly familiar passage that you would like to memorize. Cover it with the file card, and begin to repeat it, while checking yourself by uncovering a line at a time. If you get "stuck," take as little a peek as you need, to get yourself started again. You will be surprised at how much you *do* know in the familiar chapters of the Bible. Then go back over the passage again, and again. Each time you will find that more has lodged in your memory.

Son, and Holy Spirit we read about in the Bible were really all the same Person—then it had to be God the Father Himself Who died on the Cross! But what would have happened to the world during the time that God was dead!? Obviously it couldn't have been the *Father* Who was crucified. Our whole salvation, however, depends on the fact that it was *God* Who died on that Cross! If Jesus wasn't really and truly God, or if He didn't truly and really die, we are not saved, and are still in our sins, for only God could make the infinite offering. The only way all this could fit together is that the Father and the Son must be One in Their Godhead, yet distinct in Their Persons. To understand, explain, and interpret such things is the work of theology.

Then, too, the doctrine of the Trinity helps us to see that even in the very Being of the Godhead there is a sharing of mutual love. Love is something you *do,* and it is difficult to see how a God Who was only One Person all by Himself could be *love,* since He would have had no other Being of His own Nature to share with. As one theologian put it: "It is not good for *God* to be alone!" Our God, however, is a divine "Community" in Himself, a Community of shared love and joy—Father, Son, and Holy Ghost: perfectly united, yet perfectly distinct so that They can enjoy and love One Another. This too is a part of theology. Every Christian needs to have a basic theology. If you don't have a true one, you are likely to acquire a false one! A lot of speculation and false teaching goes by the name of "theology" these days, but if we remember that theology is just the attempt to sum up in an orderly and usable way what the Bible is saying about God, we won't go far wrong. As soon as theology becomes human speculation, or an intellectual game, it is worse than useless.

The briefest theological summaries are called the "creeds." Most Christians are familiar with the Apostles' Creed, not so many with the Nicene Creed. Every believer would profit by being familiar with these two statements. They are true because they agree with Scripture. They do not present the complete way of salvation to the unbeliever. They are statements for the *believer* regarding the nature of God, Christ, the Holy Spirit, the Church, etc. A third, called the Athanasian Creed, is far less known; yet it is a magnificent statement about the Trinity that would help every believer. It is true that this statement presents salvation as depending on right intellectual belief, which we know is not true—yet it would not hurt modern Christians to lean a little more in that direction! These three creeds came into existence as defenses against false teachings. Each phrase or clause affirms an important fact in the face of Satan's attempts to mislead the people of God. Today, as the Church is being renewed and brought to life in the Holy Spirit, false doctrines are again flourishing as Satan counterattacks. We may need to expand further our statements of belief as useful summaries of right teaching in the face of falsehood.

Longer and more detailed statements of theology are to be found in the confessions of the various churches: the Westminister Confession, the Augsburg Confession, the Thirty-Nine Articles are perhaps the three best known. Then there are the catechisms of the various churches. *Do not scorn or discard* out of hand these products of Christian experience. Remember the saying: "Don't throw the baby out with the bath-water!" Inspect carefully the statements of faith that your particular church has inherited. It may well be that many no longer take the confession and catechism of their churches seriously. That doesn't matter. *You* take it seriously. Study it in the light of the Scriptures, illuminated by the Holy Spirit. You will find gems of understanding that will equip you for battle. *Of course* you will find things you can't accept—that are unscriptural—but those you can reject without throwing away the whole thing. "Submit yourselves one to another in the fear of God" also includes submitting yourself to believers who came before you in history, listening to your forefathers who also knew the Lord!

This is a good time to speak of Christian reading in general. There are some excellent popular books of theology which will help you to be a better-equipped soldier in the Lord's army. Here again you need not necessarily accept everything that is written in a particular book, but if the writer is a believer, you can listen and learn, while discarding that which does not strike you as being right. The books of such men and women as C. S. Lewis, Dorothy Sayers, Andrew Murray, Watchman Nee, and a host of others will help you greatly.

The Ministry. While we are talking of the churches and their confessions, and the need for sound theology, it is a good time to talk about the ordained ministry. It is very popular today to condemn ministers along with the denominations, as if the whole were simply an artificial human organization without divine power or authority. Remember, that while God is certainly not interested in "labels," or in our human divisions, He does call men to the ministry. People grow impatient with the pastors of their dead churches and tend to turn away from them, but be careful. Many of these men were validly called of God to exercise ministry in the Church of God: elders, pastors, evangelists, apostles, prophets, teachers. They may have become entangled in the web of denominationalism, but the Holy Spirit is trying to free them. When God calls a man, He calls him. The "gifts and calling of God are without repentance," and the Scripture says that we are to respect the ministry that the Spirit has established. Listen to your pastor, even though he is not yet open to your witness about the work of the Holy Spirit. Help him, pray for him, and conform to his "Godly admonitions." Your relationship to your pastor, as long as you are a member of the congregation, is to "obey them that have the rule over you," just as the Christian wife is to obey her husband. Obviously she does not obey him in things that would be against the Lord, but she obeys him in everything she can. So with the pastor. You cannot obey him if he tells you something that is against the Word of God, but you can obey him in many things. God will bless you for it, and it may be the means of leading your minister to the baptism in the Holy Spirit.[2] If you find yourself unable to respect a minister at all, or to in any way go along with his leadership, then leave that congregation and find another. Do not be a "troublemaker." (Of course, you may be accused of troublemaking unjustly—you can't help that, but don't really and knowingly be a *rebellious* member.)

The decision whether or not to remain in a church that seems dead is one that you alone can make. Our advice is always to "stay put" if you can, as long as there is anyone listening to you. On the other hand, you can stay in an unbelieving situation only as long as you are able to make it clear that you do not agree with the wrong teachings. You cannot be put in the position of seeming to be part of it all, or you may lead others astray. If you yourself are strong enough to be uninfluenced by the teaching, you may be able to "stay put." If you have children, however, who are not yet able to protect themselves, you cannot expose them, but must find a fellowship where they can be properly nurtured. As one man put it: "If you can sit on an ice cube and melt it, stay where you are, but if it is freezing you, get off!"

Denomination. God isn't necessarily deserting the denominational churches, either. Most of the leading denominations began in deep Christian belief and fervor. They did not begin in a

---

[2] You may be in a church where the minister has not yet accepted Christ. Don't assume that because he is in the ministry, he must therefore be a believer! With a minister, just as with a lay person, always find out first what the relationship is with the Lord Jesus before going on to pray about receiving the Holy Spirit.

desire to separate, but to spread the fire of God. The Methodist movement is a good example. Wesley had no desire to separate from the Church of England, and indeed, he himself never did do so. It was the Church of England that forced the early Methodists to construct their own organization. Martin Luther had no desire to separate from Rome, but he was forced to do so by the Roman Catholic leadership of the day. Gradually, as the years went by, much of the original fervor died out, and the denomination is left trying to keep in existence for the sake of existing. "There has always been an Episcopal Church in this town, and we'll see to it that there always will be, even if only two people attend services!" As God reaches into the churches of various denominations, and brings people to life within them, denominational walls are crumbling. We must let the Holy Spirit do His work, which is the real ecumenical movement.

Don't pay attention to the "come-outers." Often with the best intentions in the world, they are simply creating new denominations that further complicate the scene. Each tradition has something to contribute to the fellowship of Christians in the Holy Spirit. Those of us who have been ministering among Roman Catholics who are receiving the baptism in the Holy Spirit are realizing what a depth of real humility and understanding of devotion is to be found among our Roman brothers and sisters; the Baptists restored to the Church the fuller symbolism of baptism by immersion; the Lutherans remind us of the standing fast in the faith; the Presbyterians, the reality of God's calling and election; the Episcopalians (Anglicans) can claim to have been used to bring the great King James Version of the Bible, for so many years the standard of the English Scriptures, and still unrivaled for literary beauty, and also the *Book of Common Prayer,* a classic of Christian devotion which should be known and loved much more widely than in the confines of one denomination. The Pentecostals, of course, brought the great witness that is reviving the Church today, the knowledge of the baptism in the Holy Spirit. It was the Methodists who reminded the English-speaking church of the most important message of all, personal salvation through Jesus Christ. And we could go on and on. God is drawing these treasures together to become a common heritage for us all.

18
The Compass

The compass. The *charts* are terribly important, but so is the *compass*, because without navigational instruments you can't follow the course line laid out on the chart. Now the compass for the Christian is *not* the Holy Spirit, but our *response* to the Holy Spirit. The compass in a ship or airplane responds to the magnetic pole of the earth, but the instrument is not always reliable. Corrections have to be made for variation, deviation, declination, etc. Thus it is important that we give attention to the accuracy of our compass, that is, that we spend much time learning how to respond more accurately to the Holy Spirit. The compass responds to the magnetic pole because it is itself magnetic. So it is the Holy Spirit in you that makes you able to respond to God. It follows that your sensitivity will increase as you allow the Holy Spirit to inspire and move you more from within. This you do through praise and prayer, and closer personal fellowship with God and experience of Him. You sensitize your own instruments by using them.

Set yourself a pattern of praise and prayer that will keep you sensitized! God created for you one purpose—that you might get to know Him personally, and have personal fellowship with Him. Heaven is the state of perfect fellowship with God, and with one another. We can have a foretaste of it here and now!

Lots of people think that God created them only to "serve" Him, in the sense of doing *chores* for Him! Recently, while we were on a "missionary journey" to far-off places, our older son came over to the house and washed and waxed the car! He didn't *have* to do it. He has a home and family of his own, living some thirty miles away. We didn't ask him to do it, or expect him to do it. He did it because he loves us. When we arrived home, Dennis didn't say to him:

"I'm glad you finally got the message! This is why I begot you —so that you could *serve* me! Now, tomorrow morning why don't you cut the lawn, and then start painting the house!"

Can you imagine us saying to our children: "We've got lots to do around here, so don't let's waste time in foolish chatter. When you come over to *serve* us, don't bother to come in the house. Just wave at us through the window. We know you love us, but the important thing is to get the *work* done!"

That's how a lot of people think about God. They think He chiefly wants them to run errands and do chores for Him, and that *that* is what is meant by "serving" God. But God really doesn't need our help in running this world—in fact, He could do it better without us, for sure. But because He loves us, He lets us share in it, just as a mother might let her three-year-old "help" her bake a cake!

God created us for His *pleasure*, the Bible says. He created us because He wanted to share His love with us. Actually, if your son came over, and offered to cut the lawn, you would be more likely to say:

"Come on in, and have a cup of coffee. Let's visit a little bit. What have you been doing lately?" And then, when you were ready, you would probably say:

"I'll come and help you cut the lawn; we can visit some more while we do it together."

This is exactly what God wants us to do: first spend a good deal of time "visiting" with Him; then go out and do the things that He lets us share in, in company with Him. "The Lord working with them," the Bible says. "We are fellow-workers together with God."

It is very hard, when we face a busy day, to spend an extra amount of time getting into fellowship with God—praising Him, and praying, and listening to what He has to say to us. It's hard to convince ourselves when we already have more to do than there is time for, that we should spend extra time with God. Yet when we are in fellowship with Him, we can accomplish many times as much; we get things in the right order; we are inspired to say and do the right things at the right time.

Make yourself a time at the beginning of the day to spend with the Lord. Start with a period that you know you can keep —it may be ten or fifteen minutes. Spend much of this time in praising God—just telling Him you love Him, and acknowledging how wonderful He is. We do not praise God because He is conceited! We praise Him because He is worthy of praise, and as we praise Him, our hearts are opened to Him to love Him more. Think of a husband coming home after work to find a delicious supper waiting for him. After the meal he will say to his wife—if he is a wise husband—"Thank you, dear, for that wonderful dinner!" That's fine! But notice that he might have said the same thing to someone he didn't even know. If he had taken his business associates to dine at a restaurant, and the meal was especially good, he might have said to the maître d': "Please convey our thanks to the chef!" He has never met the chef, and perhaps never will. You don't have to *know* someone in order to *thank* him. People thank God and are grateful to Him, who have never met Him! He has answered prayer, and in gratefulness they thank Him. It is very important to *thank* God, but it is more important to praise Him.

If the husband we talked about a little while ago really loves and appreciates his wife, he will *praise* her. He will say:

"Honey, you're a wonderful cook! In fact, you're a wonderful girl! I love you very much!" Notice that he could say this even though she had just returned from a two-week trip to visit her mother, and hadn't cooked him anything for two weeks! He isn't thanking her for something she's done, he's praising her for what she *is*. You thank someone for what he's *done,* but you praise him for what he is. It follows that in order to *praise* someone you have to *know* him.

When the husband *praises* his wife, she does not swell up with pride and say: "Well, I'm glad you recognize my worth!" No, she says to him something like: "Well, honey, I think you're pretty wonderful, too!" and love grows between them. Praise is not insincere flattery. The wife knows that her husband is telling the truth—she *is* a good cook, and she does honestly try to be a wonderful wife.

God rejoices in the love of His children, and as we praise Him, our hearts come open, not only to love Him more, but to be able to accept more freely the blessings He is ready to pour upon us. So spend much time in praising God, both privately and publicly, and your love for Him will grow. This is, of course, not separated from your inspirational use of the Bible. You will want to relate your Bible reading to your prayer and praise. Many find it helpful to begin with reading the Scripture, looking for a verse or passage that especially speaks to them, and then moving into praise and prayer.

Spend much time in speaking in tongues—let the Holy Spirit guide you to pray and praise "in the Spirit." This is very important indeed.

Offer your requests to God with confidence. There is nothing wrong with petitionary prayer (asking God for things). Jesus strongly instructed His followers to do it. He said: "Up till now you have not asked anything in My Name. Ask, and you shall receive, that your joy may be full!" (John 16:24). Remember that Jesus said you should thank God ahead of time for the answer to your prayer. Mark 11:24 says: "Whatever you ask when you are praying, believe that you receive it, and you shall have it." Don't just lamely tack "if it be Thy will" on to the end of every prayer. If you are not sure what God wants in a particular situation, then pray first of all that He will show you how to pray. Search the Scriptures to see how God feels about your need. Pray confidently, and you will see results. Confession of sin is, of course, also a part of your daily prayers. Always offer to God immediately anything in your life that has been wrong, ask His forgiveness, and *accept* it! It is as important to say, "I accept Your forgiveness, Lord," as it is to say, "I ask Your forgiveness, Lord." (Refer to pages 121 and 151, and footnotes.) Stop many times during the day and offer God praise and prayer. If you can turn completely away from your work, and get by yourself in a place where you can pray out loud, strongly and firmly, so much the better; if not, pray where you are, under your breath, but stop and praise and pray. The Scripture says: "Seven times a day do I praise Thee" (Ps. 119:164 KJV).

During the course of the day, at work or at play, try to remain sensitive to the leading of the Holy Spirit. Don't be afraid to trust His leadings, if they are in keeping with God's Word, and in "decency and order." You'll make mistakes sometimes, but God will take care of you. Actively believe Jesus to open the way for you, to meet your needs, to work miracles in your life. The Scripture says that the greatest sin is not believing in Jesus (John 16:9). This doesn't just refer to our initial belief in Him and acceptance of Him, but to our moment-by-moment trust in Him to preserve us and guide us. Whenever you find yourself dropping into worry or anxiety or upset, reaffirm your active belief in Jesus. Tell Him: "I believe! I believe! I believe that You are meeting my needs and guiding my life, right now!" Jesus said: "All things are possible to him that believeth" (Mark 9:23 KJV).

Fellowship. The Christian faith is not a solitary thing. When a certain modern philosopher defined religion as what "a man does with his solitariness," as far as Christians are concerned, he couldn't have been farther afield! The aim of God is not only to draw us to enjoy Him, but to show us how great it is to enjoy one another in Him. To enjoy God by oneself is great, but to enjoy Him in company with others is far greater—this is why the early Christians would risk their lives any time to "assemble themselves together," because when they assembled together, the glory of God was so heightened, that sometimes the very room they were meeting in would be shaken as if by an earthquake! This kind of fellowship is still available to you today. When you compare the kind of thing "going to church" has become—a kind of dull, if not unhappy, duty—with what it meant to the early Christians to get together, you will see how much we have lost track of what it is all about, but the baptism in the Holy Spirit has begun to restore this fellowship in the Lord. A "worship service" is supposed to be God's people enjoying a little foretaste of Heaven, as they share their joy in Christ with one another! They meet together to enjoy the Lord and one another in the Lord. Out of this joyful service, the gifts and fruit of the Holy Spirit proceed.

Where will I find this fellowship? If you are in a church where the pastor and perhaps many of the people know about the baptism in the Holy Spirit, there is probably a prayer meeting—or several—at which you can share in praise and prayer in the freedom of the Spirit. If so, praise God! You are very fortunate! But if your church is not like this, that does not mean you should leave. No—but it *does* mean that you need to go elsewhere to get your "spiritual food"! It means that you need to be faithful in attendance at your own church, while going to prayer meetings and Bible study somewhere else to get nourishment so you can show the joy of the Lord to your *own* church. God is not concerned with our labels; He is working in every denomination today to reach His people. He is not rejecting the old-line churches, He is working in them when He is permitted to, and if you leave your old-line church you may be deserting the work God has for you. You may discover that the group to which you go has problems, too.

God is not starting new churches and denominations today, but many human beings *are*, often with the best intentions in the world. The world is being dotted with little groups where a leader has said: "I am your apostle, and we're going to start a *New Testament* Church with *me* at the head!

In the New Testament we find the churches sharing ministry. We find prophets, apostles, evangelists, and others traveling from church to church, sharing, correcting errors, encouraging, exhorting, rebuking in the Spirit where they found something wrong. We do not find isolated fellowships living under one elder or teacher, and having nothing to do with others. We do not find men claiming absolute authority over one church or another. We find a shared ministry—submitting one to another. No one in the New Testament says: "I just get my word from the Lord." The instruction in the New Testament is: "[Submit] yourselves one to another in the fear of God" (Eph. 5:21 KJV), and we find this going on both at the level of the local assembly, and also among the leaders—even the apostles (Gal. 2).

So the most important thing you must look for when selecting a church or prayer group for fellowship, or when selecting a teacher is their *fellowship* and submission to others on as wide a basis as possible. Jude speaks of those "Who set themselves apart, soulish, not having the Spirit." (Jude 19). Paul, in Romans 16:17 (KJV), says: "Mark them which cause divisions . . . and avoid them." Do not be led astray by having some of these folk quote you: "Come out from among them and be ye separate . . .". If you will examine this verse in context, you will see that it speaks of *believers* coming out from among *unbelievers, not* brethren from brethren (II Cor. 6:17 KJV). The only time we are to separate is from unbelief—false teaching, denial of the faith—or wrong moral behavior that destroys fellowship with God.

No one can "join the church." When a person meets and receives Jesus, he becomes a part of the Church, the people of God. It is Jesus Who joins us to the Church, and the "local church" is simply all those in a given locality who have received the Lord.

If the fellowship you join, or the teacher you listen to, is submitted to others, then you are sure you will have a "balanced diet," and excesses or errors will be corrected as the Holy Spirit moves among His people. Remember, too, that you must be willing to submit to your brothers and sisters in the Lord. You must be willing to listen, and to learn. The sheep is safe as long as he stays with the flock and the Shepherd. The first thing a wolf wants to do is to get a sheep to leave the flock; then the wolf can easily devour him. There are, as Paul says, "grievous wolves" prowling around the flock of God (Acts 20:29), and the first mark of the wolf is that he wants to separate sheep from the flock and get them to himself. The most vulnerable believer is the dear soul who says, "I don't belong to any church; I just follow the Lord!" It is very hard for a sheep to follow the Shepherd without being part of the flock! If you follow the Shepherd, you are automatically going to have to be part of the flock!

Christians need fellowship. As we have said, there is nothing greater than enjoying the joy of the Lord in company with others. This is what Heaven is. Remember, though, that you can continue this fellowship with the Lord when you are not able to be with other believers. If you don't get regular fellowship, you will find it harder to keep your own freedom in the Spirit, but you *can* do it. Don't despair because you can't find fellowship, or are in a situation where for the time being you can't have it. This is why Paul tells you:

"Be filled with the Spirit, speaking *to yourselves* in psalms and hymns and spiritual songs, singing and making melody in your heart to the Lord" (Eph. 5:18–19 KJV). When you can't share fellowship in the Lord with others, you keep the fire burning in your own heart by speaking *to yourself* of the joy and glory of the Lord! Then too, the fellowship will be that much more wonderful if each member has been keeping up his individual fellowship with Jesus while he is apart from the others. Don't let down on this, and expect to get a spiritual "pick-me-up" from the meeting! If everyone comes to a prayer meeting expecting to *get* something, all are likely to go away hungry and frustrated! The blessing of the fellowship is greatest when all come with something to *share*.

Witness. In Isaiah 9:3 (KJV) the Scripture says: "They joy before Thee according to the joy in harvest . . ." and some of the greatest joy of your Christian life will come as you tell someone else about Jesus, helping Him with the harvest. If you don't witness to others about the Lord, you will not be likely to keep your own joy. One of the greatest ways to stimulate your freedom in the Spirit is to make a *personal* witness. A personal witness means telling another person "eyeball to eyeball" what Jesus means to you, personally. Pray that you may have many such opportunities. Pray that God will let you witness every day.

Wait for God to open the doors when you witness. A good witness is not necessarily rushing in and saying: "Are you saved?" or, "Do you know Jesus?" You may so frighten or offend the person that he may run away from God for years. Jesus said we were to be fishermen, and fishing is a delicate skill. So is witnessing! You may spend an hour just in casual conversation with someone, getting acquainted with him, letting them know you are a sensible, normal person, before you can even begin to move in the direction of telling him anything else. You may even have to break off the conversation the first time before getting to the point, but you will have broken the ice, and gained the person's confidence. Don't lecture! Get the other fellow to ask the questions, and don't go on and answer questions he hasn't asked!

The minute he shows the least sign of losing interest, you change the subject. If *he* changes it, he's likely to go away shaking his head, saying that you tried to stuff your religion down his throat! But if he or she shows real interest, don't be afraid to move ahead.

You will be surprised how easy it is to get a person to follow right along and accept the Lord, and the baptism in the Holy Spirit, if you are sensitive to the moving of the Spirit. The Holy Spirit will be moving ahead of you, if you are being sensitive to what He is doing—He will be opening the doors, and all you have to do is go through them! It is, after all, the Holy Ghost Who convicts the world of sin. This, by the way, should be the focus of your witness. Don't get off on discussing theology, morality, or politics—get to the point. A person is a sinner, not because of his habits, or his behavior, but because he doesn't believe in Jesus Christ (John 16:7–11).

Relax and enjoy witnessing. Don't get "up tight." Don't be a "scalp collector"! The Apostle Paul said: "I have planted, Apollos watered, but God gave the increase" (II Cor. 3:6 KJV). You may be used to speak just a few words to someone, to start things going. Someone else may actually reap the crop that you planted. That's just fine—another time you'll get to reap a crop that someone else has planted and watered!

Witness, after all, is simple enough. It's just one human being telling another about something wonderful that he has found, and that he wants to share. Up our way our young people say, "Have you had your spiritual vitamins today?" That means: "Have you told someone about Jesus today?"

Enjoy God yourself—glorify Him in your own heart; then go and tell others about Him! Remember, too, that the gifts of the Holy Spirit are given for witness—so that others can see that Jesus is really alive, and working through you. Expect God to honor you when you step out to manifest the gifts. Is the girl who works at the desk next to you looking sad this morning?

"I've got a terrible headache," she says.

What about trusting Jesus to heal her? Oh, don't pounce on her and frighten, but say something like:

"Would you mind if I prayed for your headache to go away?"

"What do you mean?"

"Oh, we believe that Jesus Christ stills heals people, like He did in the Bible, you know, and we often pray for people who are sick."

"*Jesus* heals people?" your friend might respond. "He lived 2000 years ago!"

"Well, you see, He rose from the dead, and we believe He's still with us, and still doing the sort of thing He did while He was on the earth; only now He works through people who believe in Him."

"Oh. Well, this head is splitting. I don't care what you do!"

Now—watch it! This is the time the Devil will tempt you to go overboard. You've got a fish on the line—*don't* yank it. Don't give her a sermon. Don't jump up and lay hands on her and begin to speak in tongues! Play it *cool.* Say something like:

"Well, okay, I'll pray." Be as natural as you know how. Don't even bow your head, and all that—just talk to God, quietly and simply.

"Lord, please heal Jane's head. Thank you very much."

If you feel it's all right, put your hand on her shoulder, but be careful about this. Some people don't like to be touched, you know.

What will Jesus do? He'll *heal* her, if the channel is open at all.

"Say! My head feels better!" Now's the time for lots of "cool" on your part! *Don't* say—"Well, praise the Lord!" Say something like: "That's great!" Let *her* pick up the ball. She may have to think about this quite awhile before she's ready to ask any more questions. If she turns back to her work without asking you anything else, you drop it, too. Don't start volunteering information. Don't pursue her with: "You see—I told you! Now don't you want to know more about it?" Let the Holy Spirit draw her—He will. This is perhaps the most difficult part of witnessing, knowing when *not* to say anything. Remember this is the Holy Spirit's work. You are just following along what He is doing. Without His support, you cannot lead anyone into the Kingdom.

Suppose nothing happens? Leave that to the Lord, too. I have almost never known anyone to resent or reject or react badly to a prayer for healing, whether there was any sign of results or not. Even if there is no apparent healing, because there is a block of some kind in your friend's acceptance, she may still very likely be moved by your concern, and by the fact that you would even ask to pray for her, or that you believe in prayer enough to "stick your neck out." People are so accustomed to the kind of religion in which nothing happens or is expected to happen, that they are startled when someone really believes.

Economics. Giving your money to God's work is a vital part of your life in the Spirit. Don't overlook it. God cannot bless your economic life unless it is open to Him. The Holy Spirit wants to guide and bless your pocketbook and your checkbook, just as He wants to guide and bless and fill every other part of you! We strongly recommend that you adopt the scriptural pattern of "tithing" (Gen. 28:22), that is, returning to God the "top ten percent"—the "firstfruits" of what He gives to you. If you receive one hundred dollars in income, immediately take ten dollars "off the top"; that is, before using the money for anything else, return one-tenth of it to God. This basic tithe should be given to your local congregation—your local family of God—and should not be diverted from there for other purposes. Over and above your basic tithes, you can make special gifts and offerings to the work—a favorite missionary project, or someone in need you are interested in helping. You will find that you can't outgive the Lord, and that the more generous you are with others, the more He can be generous with you.

Manner of living. Your freedom and sensitivity to the Holy

Spirit will be affected a great deal by your manner of life. Remember, too, that if you have received the baptism in the Holy Spirit, people will have their eyes on you to see how you are going to behave! Satan will be watching, too, for he knows it will be a double victory for him if he can get a baptized-in-the-Holy-Spirit Christian into disgrace. When you received the Holy Spirit, you moved into the "front line" of the Lord's Army. You began to take a more active part in spiritual battle and discovered that you had power and authority over the forces of the enemy. This of course did not make Satan, the enemy, very happy. But don't let that fact bother you; as long as you stick close to Jesus the enemy's pot shots can't touch you (I John 5:18; 4:4). Don't foolishly go wandering away from the Lord's protection! Watch your manner of life, for your own sake, and for the sake of your witness to others. The Apostle Paul said: "Abstain from all appearance of evil" (I Thess. 5:22 KJV), and that's very good advice.

The Holy Spirit does not deal at first with our specific sins and vices and bad habits. He first convicts of unbelief. The basic sin, as we have pointed out, is not believing in Jesus. When we believe in Him, and have received Him, the Holy Spirit moves on to press us to be more and more like Jesus—to change our habits of living so that we are not "conformed to this world" but "transformed by the renewing of [our] mind[s]" (Rom. 12:2 KJV). Some of this change comes quite quickly, some much more slowly. Always, Satan will be tempting us to turn back to old patterns and habits.

Some expect the process of cleanup and change to be automatic and without effort on our part. They say:

"I'll quit my bad habits when God does it for me: when He just takes them away!"

But that isn't the way it is. We have to work *with* the Holy Spirit. He never takes away our free will. We have to help Him as we purify ourselves, even as Jesus is pure (I John 3:3). Therefore it behooves the Christian to be careful of his or her manner of life. The Christian who doesn't pay his bills, who isn't quite honest in his business dealings, who quarrels noisily with his family is not going to help the cause of Christ by his behavior. The world is also going to be watching to see how you conduct yourself in lesser matters. The Christian who always looks grubby, or whose house is always a mess, to say nothing of the garden, is also making a poor witness for the Lord. The mother who isn't at home to greet her children from school, but lets them run wild in the neighborhood while she is at church, or at a prayer meeting, is not going to impress her friends with her faith. Most of this is a matter of common sense, and of asking yourself: "How would it appear to me, if I were one of the onlookers?"

Recreation and entertainment. The Bishops of the Church of England recently declared the Realm of England to be a missionary field. They recognized that their country can no longer honestly be called "Christian." It would be well for us Christians if we could realize the same thing about the U.S.A., as a whole. It would give us a better sense of perspective if we could realize that our modern culture, worldwide with its literature, art, music, customs, and morality is pagan, not Christian.

This does not mean the U.S.A. has to stay this way. The fires of the Holy Spirit are springing up in many parts of the world and in our own country. We are delighted with the fact that a number of top-notch entertainers are meeting Jesus and being baptized with the Holy Spirit, and some of their influence is already being seen in the entertainment fields.

All we are saying is, be on the alert. There's no need to make a blanket condemnation of all entertainment—movies, TV, art, music, etc.—but rather there is a need for the Christian to be very careful in selecting what of these things he or she can take part in. Don't leave the television set running all day, dribbling the thinking and attitudes of the world into your home, and into the minds of your family. Don't go to just any movie for a means of escape. Most movies today are spiritual poison. Don't subscribe to all the "regular" magazines. There are still a few left that can safely be brought into your home—select those few. Are your children believers? Do they know Jesus, and the wonderful experience of His Holy Spirit? Then you must explain and point out to them how listening to most modern "teen-age" music will take away their joy in Christ, and fill their minds with erroneous teaching. Provide them with some of the good record albums of Christian folk music and other styles of music being made available for them today.

Don't build your family life around commercial entertainment. Let it be the exception rather than the rule. Develop creative family good times: games, recreation, hobbies, outdoor activities —instead of watching TV, or going to the movies. It's safer, and a lot more fun!

Good works. You know by now that doing good things isn't what makes you a Christian, but the Bible says repeatedly that God will reward us according to what we have done. Loving your neighbor as yourself includes feeding him when he is hungry, clothing him when he is in need, visiting him when he is sick or in prison. And your neighbor isn't just the family next door, as Jesus pointed out, but whatever person in need you may come in contact with. The Apostle James says it is mockery to say to someone who is hungry and cold: "God bless you! Be warmed! Be fed!" unless you actually *do* something to help them.

Christian social action, about which so much is said today, should be simply Christians at work in the world wherever they are. The Church organization is not supposed to be a political pressure group, but Christians are supposed to take an interest in politics, and bring their convictions with them. The church organization is not supposed to be directly involved in disputes between capital and labor, but Christians who are leaders in capital and labor must bring their convictions into their confrontations. The businessman who is in Christ, will treat his employees as Jesus would treat them, and the Christian employee will give the kind of day's work that Jesus would give. "As He is, so are we in this world" (I John 4:17) is the basis of true "social action."

You and your family should also be taking part in helping God's work on a broader basis—helping to support people on the mission field, sharing in church community projects, etc. Of course you must wait on the Lord, Who will direct you in all these things, but don't use "waiting on the Lord" for an excuse for not doing them. They are a vital part of your Christian life and witness.

Cooperating with God. The word *cooperate* simply means to "work together," and the Scriptures teach that God wants us to be co-workers with Him (I Cor. 3:9; II Cor. 6:1). This means that although God has created us as free beings, He is depending on our cooperation in bringing His love to the world.

The Lord Jesus didn't write a book, though the most important Book in the world has been written about Him; He didn't travel more than a few miles from His birthplace, yet He had a plan to reach the ends of the earth. After washing away their sins, He filled His first followers with God's love, joy, and power, and sent them to pour out this joy, love, and power to others, and to tell them that they, too, could be forgiven, and filled with the glory and power of God. This is the Good News, the Gospel, and the people who hear and accept become God's people, the Church.

It is a most effective method, for if one person receives Christ today, and a greater power to witness through the baptism in the Holy Spirit, and tomorrow helps two others to receive Him, making sure that they also are baptized in the Holy Spirit, and those two each help two others to receive Him, and those four in turn each reach two others on the following day, and so forth, then in thirty-three days, nearly five billion people, the present population of the earth, would be reached!

[1] This amazing multiplication would be the case if each Christian, reached only *two* other persons for God in a life time. Obviously empowered Christians should pray for an opportunity *daily* to witness for Christ, and during their life time to win hundreds to Him.

This is the principle Jesus Christ depended upon to reach the world: each person to tell others, and they in turn to tell others, until millions all over the world are filled with the glory of God. The plan again and again has started up and then has seemed to fail, because of the unfaithfulness and forgetfulness of human beings, and the confusions and sidetracks of the enemy. Mostly it has failed because only a partial message has been transmitted: forgiveness without power. Today, however, the "full Gospel" is once again being proclaimed, not only the essential fact that God forgives and loves His people, but that having done so He empowers them to reach others. God's plan is to have millions of men and women, yes, and children, too, all over the world bringing His love and forgiveness and healing and power to mankind. We are living in the age of the revival of the Church, and it's exciting! All over the world, people are discovering how wonderful it is to tell others about Jesus and the power of the Holy Spirit, and we know God's plan is not going to fail! This may well be the last great renewal before the coming of the Lord Jesus Himself. We hope and pray that this book will help you *cooperate* with God, and that as His child and co-worker, you may continue to be filled to overflowing with His great joy.

Publisher's note:
Dennis Bennett is the author of the best-selling book,
Nine O'Clock in the Morning,
a personal account of his introduction to the life in the Holy Spirit.
Published by Logos International, Plainfield, N.J., 07060

INDEX

* n stands for footnote.

BIBLIOGRAPHY

BOOKS

Arndt, W.F. and Gingrich, F.W., eds., *A Greek-English Lexicon of the New Testament and Other Early English Literature* (Chicago: University of Chicago Press, 1957).

Bennett, Dennis, *Nine O'Clock in the Morning* (Plainfield, N.J.: Logos, 1970).

Berry, George Ricker, Ph.D., *Interlinear Greek-English New Testament* (Grand Rapids, Mich.: Zondervan, 1969).

Book of Common Prayer, The, (Philadelphia, 1789).

Brumback, Carl, *What Meaneth This?* (Gospel Publishing House, 1949).

Freeman, Hobart, *Angels of Light?* (Plainfield, N.J.: Logos, 1969).

Gasson, Raphael, *The Challenging Counterfeit* (Plainfield, N.J.: Logos, 1966).

Harper, Michael, *Spiritual Warfare* (Plainfield, N.J.: Logos, 1970).

Henry, Matthew, *Commentary on the Whole Bible* (New York: Revell) VI, 100.

Macdonald, George, *What's Mine's Mine* (New York: McKay, 1886).

Martin, W.R., *The Kingdom of the Cults* (Minneapolis: Bethany, 1965).

Nee, Watchman, *Changed Into His Likeness; Release of the Spirit; Sit, Walk, Stand* (Great Britain: The Chaucer Press, Ltd., Bungay, Suffolk, 1962).

Sherrill, John, *They Speak With Other Tongues* (New York: McGraw-Hill, 1964).

Specter, R.R., *The Bud and the Flower of Judaism* (Springfield, Mo.: Gospel Publishing House, 1955).

Wigglesworth, Smith, *Apostle of Faith; Ever Increasing Faith* (Springfield, Mo.: Gospel Publishing House, 1924).

MAGAZINES

"Indonesia: The Greatest Work of God in the World Today," *Acts Magazine* I, no. 3, 1967.

"South Pacific. Scene of Miracles Today," *Christian Life Magazine*, April, 1968.

S.W. McCurdy as told to Jamie Buckingham, "In Time for God's Appointment," *Christian Life Magazine*, October, 1969.

World Map Digest (Fontana, Calif., 1970) X, 22.